D0014757

ORGANIZATION
AND ADMINISTRATION
OF THE
LEARNING RESOURCES CENTER
IN THE COMMUNITY COLLEGE

WAUBONSEE COMMUNITY COLLEGE

ORGANIZATION AND ADMINISTRATION OF THE LEARNING RESOURCES CENTER IN THE COMMUNITY COLLEGE

Kenneth W. Allen
Waubonsee Community College

Loren Allen
Okaloosa Walton Junior College

Linnet Books · 1973

Library of Congress Cataloging in Publication Data

Allen, Kenneth W
  Organization and administration of the learning
resources center in the community college.

  Bibliography: p.
  1. Municipal university and college libraries—
Administration. 2. Instructional materials centers—
Administration. I. Allen, Loren, joint author.
II. Title.
Z675.M93A39   025.1   73-7539
ISBN 0-208-01306-7

© 1973 by The Shoe String Press, Inc.
First published 1973 as a Linnet Book
by The Shoe String Press, Inc.
Hamden, Connecticut 06514
All rights reserved
Printed in the United States of America

Contents

List of Tables

Preface

The purpose of this book is to assist community colleges in establishing and maintaining the campus learning resources center. To date there have been few if any comprehensive works which have as their primary focus the administration of the learning resources center. Therefore, the authors set out to capture relevant data and incorporate it into a unified plan for action. True, the community college must have and maintain a separate identity, but the valuable lessons learned by colleagues at the four year level and the secondary level can be incorporated into the community college.

Ten years ago, master plans incorporating a statewide system of community colleges were a reality in only a few states. Today, the community college is becoming a national movement, and it has found a place in higher education. It is our hope and desire that this work may assist persons establishing and working in the learning resources centers in the community college by giving them a base from which to proceed.

The authors would like to thank the following persons for their assistance and direction: Dr. Kenneth Shibata, Dean of Instruction, Waubonsee Community College; Professor Eileen Noonan, Graduate School of Library Science, Rosary College; Dr. Albert Donor, Dean of Instruction, Nassau Community College; Dr. Paul Libassi, Director of Institutional Research, Suffolk County Community College, and Mr. Charles Palermo, President, Laurence University.

K.W.A.
L.H.A.

Chapter I

THE NATURE OF THE COMMUNITY COLLEGE

The community college movement has been of paramount importance to the field of higher education in the past decade and its growth will certainly not diminish over the next decade. Multi-purpose, comprehensive, and inexpensive higher education is currently available in many localities for students with a diversity of ages and backgrounds. As American higher education has faced an ever increasing demand for its services, the community college has begun to provide a solution.

Although some communities have looked upon the two-year college with skeptical eyes, states such as California, New York, Texas, Illinois, Michigan, and Florida have accepted the concept readily. The recent publication by the American Association of Junior Colleges, *Junior Colleges in 50 States/50 Years,* has served notice that the community college concept has become a nationwide development.[1]

An example of this movement is represented by the State of Illinois through the development of a state-wide system of community colleges in its Master Plan for Higher Education. As a result of the Illinois Public Junior College Act of 1965, the state currently has forty-six two-year colleges providing a comprehensive educational program to meet the needs of students beyond high school.[2] During the fall of 1970, Illinois community colleges had an enrollment of 169,961 students representing a 14.8 per cent increase over the previous year.[3]

In 1971, the nation-wide enrollment figures stood at over two and one-half million students and the projections for the year

1

1980 will almost reach five million students.[4] The rise in enrollments seems to stem from two causes: the increase in the population and the demands and aspirations of American society. "The
community college became both the catalyst to stimulate a community consciousness and the product of this consciousness. The
college became a symbol of what the community, almost wistfully,
wanted to become."[5]

"The community junior college has successfully traversed the
trials of infancy and adolescence. In its maturity, it must accept
the obligation to strive for excellence at every level of its broad
scope of educational tasks. . . . As these colleges dedicate themselves to these responsibilities, they will play a major part in the
further evolution of American civilization."[6]

In developing a rationale for the organization and administration
of a learning resources center at the community college level, it is
appropriate to have a basic knowledge of the background of the
community college movement. Therefore, the remainder of this
chapter explores the literature relevant to three aspects of the
community college: (1) the nature of the student; (2) the nature
of the curriculum; and (3) the nature of the faculty.

The Nature of the Community College Student

The student population of a community college is generally composed of two distinct age groups, those from eighteen to twenty-
one and the student who is not classified as college age. Medsker
analyzed 13,000 regular day students and found that 43 per cent
were nineteen years old or younger, 10 per cent were from twenty
to twenty-two, and 47 per cent were over twenty-three years of
age. The older students typically enroll as part-time or unclassified
students. They view a course of studies as serious business and,
consequently, are more realistic in their personal and academic goals.
Medsker also found that 23 per cent of the students were married.[7]

A recent study completed by the American College Testing Program revealed that the average student had just completed high school before entering the community college and was planning to enter a four-year institution after terminating work at the two-year college. The students were found to be lower in academic potential, and they chose their institutions for practical reasons—proximity and cost. Students enrolled in vocational or occupational programs tended to be either low family socio-economic status and high aptitude or high family socio-economic status and low aptitude. They were likely to be underachievers.[8]

Blocker listed five general characteristics which are common to the community college student:

(1)   Two-year college students are, on the average, less academically able than students of four-year colleges and universities.

(2)   Two-year students, on the average, come from lower socio-economic backgrounds than do their counterparts in the four-year colleges and universities.

(3)   Two-year college students are facing the most critical period of their lives in terms of vocational choice.

(4)   A substantial number of students will continue their education at other institutions of higher learning.

(5)   The students of two-year colleges, considered as a whole, are more similar to other students of higher education than they are different.[9]

Patricia Cross indicated that a synthesis of research suggests that the following items are known about community college students:

(1)   There is an extremely high probability that any carefully designed research study will find large and diverse samples of junior college students achieving lower mean scores on academic ability tests than comparably selected samples

of four-year college and university students.

(2) . . . Parents of junior college students tend to have lower socio-economic status than parents of students entering four-year colleges and universities.

(3) Junior college students are likely to be attracted to a college for practical reasons—low cost, nearness to home, and because it offers the job training that will lead to a higher income.

(4) Intellectual interests clearly differentiate high school graduates who do not enter college, those who enter junior colleges, and those who attend four-year colleges.

(5) Junior college students do not feel as well prepared for college as four-year college students.[10]

As previously pointed out, the community college student usually does not devote all his capabilities to pursuing his college studies. Many students, in order to attend college, work outside the college on a part-time basis. The American College Testing Program found that the extent to which students worked and the number of hours they worked was unrelated to their plans, achievements, participation in school activities, and general satisfaction.[11] There are few differences between students who work and students who do not.

Community college educators record that their student population is not the same as their counterparts' in the four-year institution. What is the difference? In either situation, each student is a unique individual. One would hope that he thinks well of himself, he thinks well of others, he sees himself as a part of a world in movement—in process of becoming, he sees the value of mistakes, he develops and holds human values, and he knows no other way to live except in keeping with his values.[12] The community college student may, however, reflect a difference in the manner in which he operates on life. His home environment has probably been the chief influencing factor and has geared his activities toward success in a non-academic environment.

In analyzing the characteristics of community college students, one might ask what they want from the college, why they are on the campus, and, in turn, what the college can do for each student. Blocker, Plummer, and Richardson have listed the following:

> First, he wants visible personal identification as a college student. Peer relationship and identification is the second powerful force in the life of college-age youth. Third, the adolescent's need for status and security encourages him to seek identification with a status occupation or curriculum. Fourth, junior college students have the same motivation toward emancipation from home and parents that is so apparent among students in four-year institutions. Fifth, the student sees the junior college as a milieu in which he can live and be treated as an adult. Finally, the student comes to college in order to qualify himself for a vocation.[13]

Community college students, despite any existent differences or similarities to four-year students, face in great measure the danger of being lost as a number, a standard deviation, or plain data. While community college student bodies may be described in terms of widely varying aptitudes, socio-economic backgrounds, marital status, and ages, each student brings emotional and mental characteristics that are raw materials for the college to process.

The limitless variety of these intangible elements presents a formidable challenge to the faculty and administration of an institution that ideally wishes to be student-centered.

The foundation for developing objectives for a student-centered community college might stem from Noel McInnis' proposal that "students are a lot like people."[14] Too often we lose the concept of the unique individual and design our learning experiences to meet the specifications of data. We frequently also design experiences which seem to indicate that something is wrong with the student instead of capitalizing upon those qualities in which he excels. If the community college does not regard its students as being unique, then perhaps one of its most promising qualities will be lost, that of a *community* college.

The Nature of Curriculum and Instruction

Excellence of instruction is regarded as the hallmark of a successful community college, and the instructor interest in individual students is considered essential to good teaching. It is a major goal of these institutions to recruit teachers, develop courses and curricula creatively, and to provide the necessary support systems to assure quality instruction for all students.

Due to its "open door" policy, the public community college will serve a highly diverse student population. It is, therefore, a strongly held conviction that the curricula be appropriately diversified and relevant to the interests, abilities, and goals of the students. In addition, curricula must be sensitive to local manpower needs and the social and cultural interests of the area.

The educational objectives of community colleges are implemented through broad areas which generally parallel the program guidelines established by a state board of education. For instance, the Illinois Public Junior College Act of 1965 reads as follows: "The Class I junior college districts shall admit all students qualified to complete any one of their programs including general education, transfer, occupational, technical and terminal, as long as space for effective instruction is available."[15] Examples of this act might include the following varieties of offerings:

(1) Baccalaureate-oriented or transfer programs are offered in the liberal arts and sciences and general education curricula for transfer from the community college to a four-year college or university offering the baccalaureate degree. The degree issued is usually an associate in arts or science with majors in areas such as: art, history, English, political science, psychology, pre-education, and biology.

(2) The occupational-oriented program consists of occupational, semi-technical, and technical curricula designed to prepare students directly for employment. These programs are organized so that students may complete an organized curriculum in two years or less. The degree issued is generally an associate in applied science with majors in areas such as: automotive technology, law enforcement, secretarial science, electronics, nursing, and data processing. Certificates may be issued to students who have taken enough courses to improve or gain a skill but do not wish to complete two years of education.

(3) The adult education program offers both formal and informal learning experiences on either a credit or non-credit basis, which will help serve the cultural, civic, recreational, and educational interests of the community. Courses may include the following: pilot ground training, ceramics, chair caning, jewelry, real estate, income tax preparation, ornamental horticulture, automobile maintenance, and small engine repair.

(4) The general studies program provides developmental opportunities to help prepare individuals for admission to occupational-oriented curricula or baccalaureate curricula or for their own intrinsic value.

(5) The gifted high school senior program allows outstanding seniors an opportunity to enroll in college courses while attending high school. Credit earned in this program may be applied toward a college degree.

The community college has been designated as a comprehensive college, that is, comprehensive in course offerings. As shown above, a broad range of programs is offered in an attempt to meet the variety of needs found in the community college student population. The responsibility for initiating and maintaining a comprehensive curriculum is vested primarily in the faculty and administration, working cooperatively through the established curriculum council or council on instruction. The curriculum council should

be charged with the responsibility of providing continuous review
of existing programs and initiating new ones. The primary obligation of this council should be the improvement of instruction. It
is the responsibility of faculty, division chairmen, and academic
deans to keep abreast of developments within subject fields and to
suggest curricular improvements to the curriculum council for
formal action. Recommendations for change are usually channeled
from the committee to the administrative cabinet and finally to
the board of trustees.

The membership of the council is representative of the institution,
and it usually includes the following members: dean of instruction;
administrative representatives of the adult education, baccalaureate,
occupational, and summer session programs; the director of the
learning resources center; a counselor; the division chairmen; and
representatives from the faculty. More and more frequently institutions are including students as members of the council with voting
privileges. B. Lamar Johnson might include one additional council
member, a vice-president in charge of heresy.

This proposal would provide a staff member—with no administrative responsibility—whose duty it would be to keep abreast
of national developments and to initiate plans for exploiting them
at his own institution, as well as to develop completely new plans
for local use and application. Our vice-president would be a
"dreamer." He would attend conferences and assemble "far out"
proposals. He would needle administrators and his faculty colleagues and, in turn, be needled by them. He would study findings of research and analyze their implications for his college.
He would, in short, be a harbinger and instigator of change.[16]

There is little doubt that a member of this stature would add his
expertise exploring different possibilities for instruction.

The personality of the community college is shaped by the nature of its curriculum and instruction. If the institution is to be a dynamic forum for learning, then so must the curriculum and its instructional implementation. The community college must commit itself to continuous self-examination, experimentation, and communication both within the institutional system and with the students for whom the system exists.

The Nature of the Faculty

The faculty found within the community college perhaps have as diverse backgrounds as the students they instruct. They range in experience and degrees from a doctorate to no degree and extensive experience to no experience. In a discussion about the preparation of community college teachers, Gleazer notes there is at least one common denominator, "an understanding of the assignment of the comprehensive community college, and sufficient acceptance of this concept to contribute purposefully and constructively toward its goals."[17] However, Blocker indicates that the greatest delay in two-year college development is a confusion as to what standards should be used in the selection and training of junior college instructors.[18] More and more graduate institutions are recognizing this as an area for instruction and are offering degrees emphasizing community college teaching including internships in community colleges in close proximity to the graduate institution.

A national study of teacher supply and demand reported that 30 per cent of the new junior college teachers came directly from high school classrooms, 17 per cent from college and university teaching, 24 per cent from graduate school, and slightly over 11 per cent from business occupations.[19]

Medsker found that more than 64 per cent of the full-time staff had once taught at the secondary or elementary school level. He also found that 9.7 per cent of the faculty held a doctorate, 64.6 per cent a master's degree, 17 per cent a bachelor's degree, and

6.8 per cent held no degree.[20] As more and more teachers are prepared for teaching in the community college, no doubt these figures will be modified.

In discussing the community college instructor, Cohen and Brower list maturity as a chief attribute of his teaching.

> The instructor is the focal point. His institution's success, the maturity of his profession, and the learning achieved by the students with whom he interacts are his responsibility. The professional associations, the administrators, and the supervisors are important to the instructor because they affect his life. But in the final analysis, he must take charge of his own affairs.[21]

The instructor needs to constantly assess himself by asking the question, "Who am I?" for the success of the institution will be reflected by the instructors who in turn will be measured by the successes of their students.

In conclusion, "the typical junior college faculty member is an individual who has adequate-to-superior preparation and personal perceptions of the middle and upper-lower class."[22] Those teachers who stand out among their peers have two characteristics in common: they are keenly and obviously interested in and enthusiastic about their subject matter, and they are thoroughly prepared.[23]

Summary

The purpose of this chapter was to serve as an introduction by describing the nature of the students, the faculty, and the curriculum. The philosophy of the community college allows it to deal with the individual by offering a wide variety of programs. By implementing its comprehensive curriculum, the community college attempts to assist today's citizen toward a fuller realization of his potential. It is the goal of education in the community college to provide a responsive environment in which students and faculty can interact and freely grow, both emotionally and intellectually.

Community college structures are proliferating rapidly, but despite the rush to put them into operation, techniques and practices cannot and should not be adopted in whole from secondary and four-year institutions. There are differences in philosophy between these two levels of public education as well as differences in their relationship to the community college. The community college is and should remain student-centered with its roots in the community. It should evolve by itself and not be burdened by the traditionalism of other educational institutions. The community college should evolute its own destiny and the newly emerging programs which are instituted must be faithfully evaluated and modified in order to meet the needs of students currently living in a democratic society. Programs which include the ingredients of excellence must be provided for all students.

Chapter II

PHILOSOPHY AND ORGANIZATION

The success of the community college will be determined by the quality of instruction provided for its clientele, the students. While each student must provide the initial motivation to learn, each one also has his own personal requirements for learning. Consequently, the environment of the institution must be one that can respond to as many combinations of aptitudes, abilities, desires to learn, and methods of instruction as there are students. Such a climate involves a highly individualized approach to learning which serves as the purpose, the method, and the criteria for evaluation of instruction, and an equally comprehensive commitment on the part of students, faculty, and administration is required.

The learning resources center as developed in this book places primary emphasis upon meeting the needs of the students within a changing environment, the community. It is the purpose of this chapter to suggest a philosophy for the learning resources center and an organizational pattern for implementing its functions.

Philosophy

The rationale for merging the library and audiovisual facilities into a single unit, the learning resources center, is based upon several assumptions. First, as society develops and grows more complex and media-oriented, no one particular format for communication can be considered as the most appropriate for all. Communication today requires a wide range of materials for students and faculty members in a variety of formats.

Second, as materials and services become more accessible, the potential for use, and, in turn, the potential for learning becomes greater. The recent recommendations of the survey on community colleges in the state of Illinois indicate that "the learning resources center should be administered as one unit under a single director."[1] The survey also states that 75.5 per cent of the participating colleges were currently administering the library and audiovisual services as a single unit.[2] Therefore, combined services with a single head, the director of learning resources, an interfiled main card catalog, and close proximity of print and nonprint materials indicate that the learning resources center concept is being adopted by community colleges because better services are provided for students and faculty if all media are coordinated and administered by one department.

Third, a very practical factor is that of control. Many colleges who have not adopted a single administrative unit have found their materials and equipment scattered throughout the complex, leading to much duplication and lack of accessibility by students and faculty.

The learning resources center has two primary functions, service and instruction. Service involves the provision of whatever materials, equipment, assistance, and guidance are required by the user. The function of instruction is implemented through assisting the student to inquire, to search, and to find a commitment to make his true education a reality. The faculty has to be aware of the opportunities available to their students and themselves through a unified facility. The more knowledge and understanding the students and faculty have of the learning resources center facilities, the more likely they will utilize and rely upon their resources.

The learning resources center concept is relatively new, and our colleges and universities, for the most part, are still teaching and using the printed media as a separate and distinct learning process. The director of the learning resources center and his staff have an additional duty, that of teaching students and faculty how to search for and use all the media that has been coordinated into one effective unit, the learning resources center. It is a continuing process that requires time, patience, understanding of faculty and students, a good knowledge of curriculum, and good professional personnel. The library ". . . is best qualified to teach that 'half of knowledge that is knowing where to find it.' And as for the other half, it is the only teaching unit in the college which can provide an unlimited interdisciplinary approach to knowledge."[3] "Whether it is called materials center, curriculum laboratory, or learning resources library, its purpose is to help create a richer learning environment through providing learning materials, experiences, and resources."[4]

As guidelines are constructed for the community college learning resources center, more and more emphasis is being placed upon the unified media concept. For example, according to the recently published guidelines, "responsibilities for all learning resources and services should be assigned to a central administrative unit."[5]

In 1969 a joint committee of the American Association of School Librarians and the Department of Audiovisual Instruction of the National Education Association prepared standards for school media programs.

The philosophy of a unified program of audiovisual and printed services and resources in the individual school is one that has continuously grown and been strengthened in the last thirty years. This fusion of media resources and services provides optimum service for students and teachers. Many schools now have unified media programs. For those others that have separate audiovisual departments and school libraries, it is recommended that, wherever possible, these services be combined, administratively and organizationally, to form a unified media program. New schools should start with a unified media center and program of services.[6]

In a discussion concerning the relationship of the library to other information resources, Duprey states:

> There is great similarity in the missions and services of academically useful resources of information in book forms, and those of academically useful resources in other forms, such as the audiovisual media. At the present, on too many campuses there appears to be unnecessary competition and duplication of effort between book libraries, on the one hand, and those specialists who are involved in what is often called "instructional services" on the other.[7]

"Modern instructional practices in education do not entail a conflict between new media and printed materials; the requirement is to fit the various media together in an ordered pattern that will make optimum use of their complementary functions."[8]

Len Singer, in describing the learning resources division at Florida Atlantic University, indicated that there are two primary functions. The first function is "to put at the disposal of the teaching faculty all media, technology, services, and systems which will enhance the effective communication of ideas in the preprogrammed phase of learning."[9]

The learning resources center is no longer a passive agent within the institution; it is dynamic and changing. The traditional library is disappearing along with separate facilities for library and audiovisual activities. These services have not always been harmonious within institutions, but they must become so if the community colleges are to fulfill their objectives.

As mentioned above, the success on one hand will result as a total integration of services; however, total success will only be obtained through taking the services to the faculty and students. It is necessary that faculty members and students understand the function and the services available from the learning resources center.

Only through cooperative efforts will the contribution of the center to the teaching situation be maximized. "Recognition must be given to the fact that use of the library is ultimately dependent upon the character of the teaching done in the classrooms and laboratories of a college."[10] That which holds true for the library certainly applies to the learning resources center concept. The community college prides itself on excellence in instruction; the center has to exert its role in effective leadership.

Organization

The nature and scope of the services to be implemented by the learning resources center will be affected by the organization of this administrative unit. The center as we have proposed in the foregoing pages should have as its chief administrator a person who is knowledgeable in at least four areas: library, audiovisual, curriculum, and management. The problems which will confront this unit will be of such a nature that a background of training and experience in these areas will be a necessity. T. N. Duprey has listed three principal problem areas as the following:

(1)   The first concerns structure, coordination of activities, and functional relationships within the learning resources center and other activities on the campus.
(2)   The proper use and coordination of non-book media with book media in the learning process.
(3)   There are few trained specialists who are also good managers with knowledge, experience and understanding of both areas.[11]

Fred Harcleroad in *Library Trends* reported that "At the present time, however, the most promising organizational developments using learning resources are taking place outside the library in large research universities, and in a new division of education services or learning resources which includes the library in smaller, instructionally oriented colleges and community colleges."[12] One of his organizational charts includes the following: an executive dean of learning resources who is responsible to the vice president for academic affairs. Under the executive dean are located the following services: libraries, independent study center, utilization or consultation services, audiovisual distribution services, materials preparation services, instructional television and radio, instructional publications services, museum services, and college or university press.

The plan seems quite acceptable for a large university; however, for the community college some deletions (college or university press) and some combinations perhaps should occur. For instance in the small or middle sized community college, the audiovisual services may be more unified, perhaps including the reading and language laboratories.

Therefore, a restructuring of the organizational plan for the community college seems appropriate. For a suggested plan of organization see Table 1. The plan serves as the overall administrative organization for the remainder of this text. Although this model is not currently utilized in all community colleges, it is a basic design from which modifications can be made.

The dean or director of learning resources is responsible to the dean or vice president of instruction. If the institution is administratively organized with a vice-president in charge of instruction, then the chief administrative officer of the learning resources center would be a dean; however, if the instruction is organized with a dean of instruction, the chief administrative office of the learning resources center would be called a director. Throughout the United States, the community colleges have established various patterns of organization, and therefore the titles of the chief administrative officer of the learning resources center vary. (See

Appendix A for position descriptions of the director and coordinators of libraries and audiovisual services.)

A common practice in the community college is to set up an advisory committee for the learning resources center. It is the duty of this committee to represent the different divisions of the college and the student body, thus allowing one channel of communication between these forces and the center. It is recommended that at least one student serve on the advisory committee. The director should serve as committee chairman. Alternative methods for establishing the committee may include: appointment by the president; appointment by the dean; election or appointment by the faculty, either directly or through a faculty committee or selection by the head of the learning resources center. The function of the committee is advisory, and it is important that the committee not concern itself with the details of daily administration.

The self-instructional laboratory, as one unit of the center, is directly responsible to the dean or director. The independent study concept is receiving increased attention in the community college. One phase of this concept is a laboratory where students can utilize materials and equipment for individualized learning. The direction of this laboratory should be under a person with knowledge in the areas of both print and nonprint media, since a variety of materials will be utilized for effective integration of curricular needs. The self-instructional laboratory should be housed as a part of the center for easy access by both students and faculty, and should be staffed by teaching personnel from the different disciplines as well as paraprofessional staff. In many cases this area is coordinated and integrated with a diagnostic center for learning difficulties. However, do not confuse the self-instructional laboratory with independent study projects which may be more appropriately housed in other areas of the college in close proximity to the appropriate physical facilities. For example, independent study facilities in automotive technology should be housed in the vocational facility where the students can receive "hands on" experience.

Table 1

ORGANIZATIONAL CHART

| | Dean or Vice President of Instruction | Advisory Committee |
| | Dean or Dir. of Learning Resourc. | Self Instructional Lab. |

Reading Lab

Language Lab

Coordinator of Audiovisual

Technician Curricula

Coordinator of Library

Faculty Library

Evening Librarians

Faculty Services (Duplication)

Instruc-tional TV

Production of Materials

Distribution of Materials

Refer-ence

Technical Services

Circula-tion

Acquis. and Serials

Both the coordinator of library services and the coordinator of audiovisual services should be under direct supervision of the director. Both have total responsibility for their respective areas and have parallel positions in the organizational scheme. For the total development of the learning resources center concept, the coordinators of both areas must work cooperatively in achieving the objectives of the center. Some colleges have totally merged the responsibilities and have not separated the traditional audiovisual and library services in the learning resources center: for instance, technical services include both print and nonprint materials, and circulation includes all materials and equipment. The intershelving of all items in the center may require alternative organization structures.

The coordinator of audiovisual services is responsible for the organization and administration of duplicating services, instructional television, the production of nonprint materials, and the distribution of nonprint materials and equipment. To begin with most of these activities will result from the servicing of faculty requests; however, student requests will multiply as the concept becomes accepted within the institution. Some institutions feel that the faculty services and materials production should be closely integrated allowing a faculty member or student to come to a single location to have materials produced, utilizing the expertise of the personnel in both areas. Also, a note should be made that, in some instances the instructional television facility may be separate from the audiovisual facility and equal to it in line relationship, depending upon the size of the institution and the emphasis placed upon it. Two auxiliary services, because of their relationship to the audiovisual complex, are the language laboratory and the reading laboratory. It is recommended that these units be coordinated and located within the learning resources center since the production of materials and maintenance of equipment are vital functions in their effective operation.

The coordinator of library services has as his responsibility the administration and operation of the library, including the acquisition, cataloging and circulation of print and nonprint materials. Reference and technical services, circulation and acquisitions, and serials activities are under his direct supervision. Some centers employ professional evening librarians from the neighboring institutions and public libraries to staff their evening programs; this allows closer articulation between these agencies and the community college. Another duty of the library coordinator is the maintenance of a faculty library. It is his responsibility to see that appropriate materials are purchased and processed for the faculty.

Many colleges are implementing curricula designed to train audiovisual and library technicians. The responsibilities of initiating and administering such a program can fall within the realm of the dean of instruction and be delegated to the director of the learning resources center. While nationally there is concern for the administration of these programs, it is recommended that the learning resources center be given responsibility for directing these programs and that a cooperative spirit exist to allow the students to receive the most appropriate learning experiences. The center itself serves as an excellent laboratory for the students to gain practical, on-the-job experience.

Summary

In this chapter a plan has been initiated for integrating audiovisual and library services under a single administrative unit, the learning resources center. The philosophy of the center is twofold: (1) the servicing of faculty and student needs; and (2) the stimulation of faculty and students toward integrating individualized instruction within the community college curriculum. Through this single administrative unit, all formats of communication media

would be organized and administered. Let it be understood that
the guidelines set forth in this chapter should be modified according to the local institution and the philosophy of service that it
provides.

In the remaining chapters, this organizational plan will be emphasized when discussing staffing, budgeting, processing, and planning. The plan will serve as a tool to integrate the goals and efforts
of the curriculum, the students, and the faculty.

Chapter III

ADMINISTRATION AND PERSONNEL REQUIREMENTS

The efficiency and success of the learning resources center in meeting its desired goals will be dependent upon the quality of staff it employs, and upon the internal and external communication system that is established throughout the organization. That is, the internal climate may accelerate or hinder the working and communicative relationship of the employees. Each professional staff member within the system will be required to fulfill administrative functions within the center in order to carry out his assigned duties. "The unique task of administration, at least with respect to staff relations, is just this: to integrate the demands of the institution and the demands of the staff members in a way that is organizationally productive and individually fulfilling."[1]

Achieving the institutional and learning resources center's objectives will require the cooperation of each individual within the system. Each person must feel his own individual worth in the environment. The individual must in his position grow intellectually and emotionally. For self-fulfillment in a position, the following is desired: "What we must reach for is a conception of perpetual self-discovery, perpetual reshaping to realize one's best self, to be the person one could be."[2] According to John Gardner, the success of the organization is achieved in terms of the role of each individual who participates and his perceptions of himself in this role.

The principles of management are essential in the attainment of a common goal within the institution. It is the responsibility of the president, the dean, the director, and also the technician. "Management is essentially the same process in all forms of enterprise at all

23

levels of organization, although the goals and environment of management may differ considerably. This simple truth is basic to understanding the principles of management."[3] These principles are not
absolute, but can be modified according to certain conditions and
can be directly applied to the operation and management of the
center.

Henri Fayol has listed fourteen principles of management which
can serve as a guideline for effective operation. They are as follows:
(1) division of work; (2) authority and responsibility; (3) discipline;
(4) unity of command; (5) unity of direction; (6) subordination;
(7) remuneration; (8) centralization; (9) scalar chain; (10) order;
(11) equity; (12) stability of tenure; (13) initiative; and (14) esprit
de corps.[4]

The work of the organization is carried out through effective
communication. The communicative channels not only flow downward but upward and horizontally. Communication is based upon
the concept of trust. The lack of trust can keep subordinates from
communicating with their supervisor and inhibit the process. If a
mutual understanding and cooperation exists, then barriers will
be reduced or minimized. However, in every organization some
barriers will still be present. To minimize these restrictions the
following factors should be considered: "(1) preventing downward
channels of communication from being overloaded; (2) encouraging
the free flow of ideas and information in all directions; (3) developing a sensitivity among members of the administrative staff to the
need for understanding the psychological barriers to effective communication; and (4) planning programs to help members of the
administrative staff with some of the fundamental problems of
communication with which they are confronted."[5] Instead of always referring decisions to the top of the organization, the collec-
tive group can and should be involved in the communication process.
For example general functions which groups might perform include
the following: planning, appraising, advising, and educating.

"Group productivity depends upon many things, including the competency of its members, the nature of the task with which it is confronted, the processes employed in the conduct of the work, the extent to which groups are permitted to use initiative in solving problems, and administrative integrity in dealing with group suggestions, decisions, or recommendations."[6]

Also within the communication system of the organization lies an informal system that perhaps is more efficient and effective than the formal channels. Edward T. Hall has made reference to this system in his book, *The Silent Language*. "We must never assume that we are fully aware of what we communicate to someone else. There exist in the world today tremendous distortions in meaning as men try to communicate with one another. The job of achieving understanding and insight into mental processes of others is much more difficult and the situation more serious than most of us care to admit."[7]

The personnel within the community college learning resources center need careful attention. A general discussion of management and the communication process, two vital elements to the center's operation, have been presented. Unless these factors are carefully considered in administering the learning resources center, much time and effort will be wasted in attempting to provide excellence. The remainder of this chapter will consist of a discussion of general elements concerning personnel and the role of professional positions in the center.

Personnel

The learning resources center requires a broadly educated and well-qualified staff in the area of communication. Familiarity with both print and nonprint media and their implications and effectiveness in the process of communication is a necessity. Furthermore, the community college media personnel needs an understanding of

student and faculty characteristics at the local institution, including
the baccalaureate and occupational as well as the adult education
curricula. The role of the professional as well as the semi-professional staff members must be understood in order to effectively serve
the students and faculty. The success of the operation in meeting
the objectives of the institution requires a well-qualified and
numerically adequate staff. "The student body, faculty, and public
using the library are peculiarly sensitive to its oversight, judgment,
and enterprise."[8]

The Director of Learning Resources

To date, the position of director of a community college learning
resources center is usually filled by a person from the library field
since most administrators still perceive the library as a necessary but
traditional fixture on the college campus. The library has often
been said to be the heart of the college and few educators will
doubt its need, yet the audiovisual aspect of learning resources is
still in stages of infancy and has perhaps not yet achieved the
same stature. However, the director should be a knowledgeable
person in both areas, that of library and audiovisual.

The specialist should have the following backgrounds:

(1) Have a knowledge of curriculum theory and of the dynamic
    of curriculum change and development.
(2) Have a background of successful teaching.
(3) Be able to communicate ideas clearly.
(4) Be able to delegate responsibilities.
(5) Have the ability to initiate interaction.
(6) Be a communicator, interpreter, and promoter of research.
(7) Have a knowledge of classification and cataloging pro-
    cedures and the ability to implement them.
(8) Be professionally prepared and aggressive enough to acquire
    that status . . .

(9)   Maintain intellectual curiosity and display a willingness to keep abreast of new developments . . .

(10)   Have a knowledge of building design and facilities . . .

(11)   Be able to work effectively with individuals and with groups.[9]

Thus, the director needs to be a leader and a communicator with knowledge areas in the field of curriculum theory, communication, library, audiovisual, and learning theory. He also needs to know how to work with others and to gain their respect.

James Brown has indicated that a media generalist could provide leadership in the area. This generalist would have the following qualifications:

(1)   a professional resource person for teachers first and fore-most; for media center professional and paraprofessional staff, for administrators, and for students.

(2)   a knowledgeable curriculum worker . . .

(3)   an administrator

(4)   a professional practitioner . . .

(5)   a catalyst for innovation and for the extension of practices of proven worth, a student of the process of educational change and especially of human relations and motivations . . .[10]

C. Walter Stone, in a recent issue of *Library Trends*, stated:

In the future, the competence of those performing the library function will no longer be measured in terms of specific media backgrounds as such but in terms of subject mastery and com-munications expertise. Needed to manage library services in the future will be several new classes of personnel including special-ists in communications analysis, production, packaging, and evaluation; systems designers and analysts; and dynamic distributive program administrators. All must be thoroughly familiar with ways in which the various forms of recorded knowledge can be acquired, stored, retrieved, distributed, and used with maximum effectiveness.[11]

In these areas, Wyman has addressed himself to the question by asking, "Whose Empire?"

We do need two new professional people who have not yet appeared on the scene in any appreciable numbers. We need a specialist in presentation design and techniques, and a specialist in individual study design and techniques . . . Audiovisual people would most likely move into the presentation area as they learned about producing presentations, group dynamics, research design, room construction, etc. Librarians would most likely move into the individual study area as they learned about newer media used in individual study carrels, evaluation, guidance, and particularly programmed instruction.[12]

In assessing who shall become the director or what appropriate field will lead in this direction, two important factors or stereotypes follow regarding the field of library science and audiovisual education. ". . . there is still among too many librarians a lack of certainty regarding optimum contributions which can be made to the process of education through uses of newer communication media including graphic and photographic materials, recordings, educational radio and TV, programmed instruction, and computers."[13] "Acceptance of the media specialist as something more than a 'woolly minded gadgeteer' won't be easily achieved. The traditional audiovisual concept cannot be considered a discipline in and of itself. Perhaps status will be more readily extended to the media specialists when other disciplines have been involved in his professional preparation."[14] A successful director for a community college should not fit either description.

There is little agreement upon what prior training is needed for the position of director. There are few if any programs that attempt to train a person for this position. Norman Tanis suggests that perhaps one of the most fruitful processes for educating a person who seeks to become a director and who has experience in related areas would be an examination of community colleges across the nation. "Further, I think the education of the junior college head librarians must lead them to an examination of excellent junior college libraries across the country . . . There is no laboratory that can teach more than the actual working library viewed and examined from day to day by an objective observer."[15]

The duties of the director will vary according to the institution in which he serves. His role can be major or minor in regard to instruction; but his primary responsibility is the administration and integration of the learning resources center with the institution's objectives. The director's duties can be identified by studying the organizational chart in Chapter II, and in the specific job description found in Appendix A. One of the director's roles is the supervision of professional, paraprofessional, and clerical staff. These relationships will next be explored.

Professional and Supportive Staff

The staff of the learning resources center can be divided into two categories. Although persons in both categories share some duties, the responsibility factor will vary considerably. The professional staff includes those persons who have advanced degrees, have considerable responsibility, understand the objectives, functions and operations of the unit, and are involved in an instructional position. Asheim, for instance, notes that the term librarian is used "to designate those who are qualified by background and training to go beyond the level of application of established rules and techniques to the analysis of library problems and the formulation of original and creative solutions for them."[16]

On the audiovisual side, Jim Wallington has asserted that the differentiation of duties is somewhat a problem. "Professional media specialists are generally acknowledged to be professionals by their relationship to the main task, instruction, not by their relationship to media . . . If we can sort out professional and non-professional personnel in instructional media, we should be able to do so by defining professional tasks—'professional,'—again in terms of instruction. If our media specialist spends all his time planning or administering programs of mediated instruction, he is usually classed as a professional." He continued: "If all of his time is spent producing (actual and physical preparation, not designing) materials, he is generally rated nonprofessional."[17]*

Swartout offers a distinction based upon three qualifications. They are: "(a) the range and depth of media competencies gained through experience, (b) the amount of formal education, and (c) the qualification to teach."[18]

Each institution must determine its own personnel classification in terms of scope of responsibility and qualifications. Classifications within the learning resources center should be in harmony with comparable positions within the community college and should not stand apart from the institutional guidelines or personnel. However, each person in the system must feel that he is wanted and is fulfilling an important and responsible role in the operation. Upward mobility within the system is important for each employee.

The standards for school media programs also point out that the job structure is hierarchical in nature.

The very fact of this assumption should communicate the urgent need to make the necessary job analyses on which to base this hierarchy and to stabilize identified positions through professional certificates or nonprofessional civil service classifications. To

*Although positions are often classified as nonprofessional in the literature the classification is absurd. The person himself will make the determination through his work and relationship with others whether he merits the classification.

do these things, professionals especially will have to examine each aspect of their present work and subject it, eventually, to the test of the question: Does this task require professional judgment or skill? Could it be done as well—perhaps better—by noncertificated personnel?[19]

Although job classifications and position descriptions are a necessity in the community college learning resources center, one cannot administer the operation without the cooperation of all staff members. The position within the organization framework should not provide a barrier of status between employees. "Recognition and definition of the diversity of roles for which personnel should be prepared; design of specific and relevant training plans for each of these roles; provision of program elements which serve to make explicit the interrelationships among these roles—[should work] to the end of establishing a continuous and integrated program for all library personnel."[20]

In the remainder of this chapter, the subject of personnel will be treated in the library and audiovisual areas respectively.

Library Personnel

The library is a major element of the learning resources center. The staff which performs functions closely allied to this area is discussed below. However no attempt is made to discuss clerical positions.

Asheim has proposed a classification for libraries consisting of three subprofessional levels and two professional levels.[21] Each position denotes a specific career ladder for the organization. In the subprofessional classifications, he has proposed that the technical assistant include the graduates of two-year college programs and that the library assistants include those with a baccalaureate degree. The professional classifications include professional specialists and librarians.

The need for a professional specialist might be questioned in the community college unless the college has substantial funds, or the specialist has training in the philosophy of the community college instead of specific subject matter.

The librarian has to be a teacher for while he is managing he is also involved vitally in instruction. Through his efforts he co-ordinates the efforts of the faculty and the available resources into a single unit. Knowledge of the community college is a necessity. "Since the junior college is treated as a segment of higher educa-tion, most library educators feel that preparation for junior college librarianship should in essence be the same as that for senior col-lege librarianship."[22] Veit reflects that a knowledge of the com-munity college setting is necessary. Unfortunately, the librarian may forget his role in instruction and allocate more time to ad-ministrative duties.

> Most librarians are overburdened with administrative detail, while at the same time few adequately cover the real admini-strative functions . . . formulating overall objectives and policies; planning; determining the organizational framework; making major decisions, including those on personnel; supervising the "middle management" heads, and seeing that they carry well the responsibilities delegated to them; balancing and co-ordinating all the workers and activities into a smoothly operating whole, and evaluating what is going on.[23]

As noted earlier, there are few agreed upon qualifications that are necessary for the community college librarian. The most necessary attributes to the position are a fundamental knowledge of librarianship, knowledge of the community college movement, successful teaching experience, and a willingness and cooperative attitude toward faculty, students, and other staff members of the center. The position requires delegation and supervision. The librarian needs the qualities of leadership, good judgment, initiative, intellectual curiosity, and resourcefulness. The success or failure of the person will be largely determined by his successful or unsuccessful efforts in working with others inside and outside the center. Thus the librarian should be hired because of his composite qualifications and not because he has a master's degree in librarianship and likes books!

Elizabeth Martin conducted a survey of community college library staffing needs and the preparation of personnel during 1966-67. She found that the respondents had little agreement upon the definition of terms such as professional librarian, semi-professional librarian, technician and untrained staff. The respondents also indicated that there was little agreement as to the training and background needed for each classification. She found that (1) under-staffing is more often due to lack of funds than to shortage of applicants; (2) job descriptions and positions have not been clearly defined; (3) specialized training in the audiovisual field is needed; (4) there is need for experience, and (5) management courses in personnel are needed.[24]

The trained paraprofessional is another element of the library staff and includes those persons referred to as the "library assistant" and the "technical assistant." The library assistant, as noted earlier, usually has a four-year degree and duties which may vary considerably. The library technical assistant has emerged from the community college. "The impact of the junior college on this innovation in personnel is evidenced by the fact that almost all of the education for this new career has occurred in the two-year institutions."[25] The library technical assistant performs diverse tasks depending upon the specific institution, but national efforts are being made to further clarify the position. Usually the position of technical assistant consists of nonroutine tasks and may require considerable judgment in performing the assigned duties. An understanding of the functions of the operation of the center and the knowledge to respond to users' requests are a necessity for the technician. "Whether a library staff member who works in a supportive capacity is to be viewed as a clerk or as a library technical assistant will depend largely in the complexity of his job, on his understanding of library procedures, and on the amount of responsibility he carries."[26]

The organization of the library element of the learning resources center may vary according to each institution as illustrated by the preceding discussion. Its success will depend upon the manner in which these positions interact since there is no absolute formula for success.

Audiovisual Personnel

The audiovisual element of the center will be discussed in terms of general requirements for personnel. The hierarchical arrangement which exists within the library field does not exist to the same degree in the audiovisual field. Broadly classified the positions consist of professional and technical. In the literature concerning the preparation of audiovisual personnel, little is found regarding nonprofessional personnel, yet they are politely and justly referred to as technicians.

"The fundamental responsibilities of the media specialist or district director are divided into three areas: administrative, supervisory, and technical."[27] More is written specifically about his relationship with other personnel outside the center, such as faculty and administration. "The media man's activities in other areas will result in a necessary realignment of relationships with other personnel, especially other administrators: administrative arrangements must be made to permit operation within the previously mentioned areas, and in addition to such policies or operating procedures, the media man must prove he is competent not only in the area of media, but also in curriculum, learning, and supervision."[28] The relationships tend to be shifted from the internal organization, the center, to external, the campus community. A major consideration becomes learning and not an organizational hierarchy of personnel. This is not to say that proper organization arrangements are unnecessary, but learning and instruction are paramount in the community college.

Dale Hamreus has proposed a three-dimensional structure for organizing media-related training requirements. One of the dimensions is aligned to responsibilities that media personnel assume in performing their duties and is thus designated as responsibility grouping.

The directive-administrative grouping includes job activities that represent top administrative and management responsibilities necessary to control media operations; the professional grouping includes job activities that are responsible to work directly in the use of media with learners and learning problems, e.g., teachers and instructional designers, etc.; the artistic-production grouping represents job activities that are responsible to work directly in the creation and production of media in support of professional type activities, e.g., graphic artist, photographer, etc. The technical grouping represents job activities that are responsible to work directly with the design, fabrication, technical adjustment, and operation of mediating devices required in instruction in support of the professional type activities, e.g., TV cameramen, technical processor, etc. . . .[29]

There is no consensus among audiovisual educators as to a model program for training the professional. Carlton Erickson has asked the following questions concerning their education:

(1) What specific and essential functions should broadly prepared media specialists be able to carry out? (2) Can the necessary audiovisual media abilities be acquired by piling audiovisual media courses on top of print-media program? (3) Should the new media

specialist be required to have taught on a full-time contractual basis for a specified number of years before attaining certification? . . . If predictions for the next decade materialize, it will not be easy to staff the schools with media specialists, especially if we are not willing to experiment with the processes of recruiting and preparing them for the services that will have to be provided.[30]

To fulfill his responsibility, the media person must spend his time working with classroom teachers in selection of materials and effective utilization of these materials. ". . . we also share our concern about the lack of competent, well-trained materials specialists to do the job that they should be employed to do—help the classroom teacher teach as effectively as possible."[31] Relative to professional training for educational television, Vernon Bronson said, "More often than not, the preparation is obtained through on-the-job training with existing status. Personnel on the educational side of these technologies are usually prepared by circumstance or expediency, which leaves much to be desired in educational expertise."[32]

As previously noted, there is little consistency concerning the requirements of or preparation for a professional audiovisual position at the community college level. Although a professional audiovisualist needs to understand the process of communication, teaching, supervision, learning theory, curriculum, and the audiovisual field, there are as yet only a few programs at the graduate level which attempt to meet the needs of the community college in this field. For the present, personnel recruitment will continue to draw from the already established community colleges. Since for audiovisual personnel operating in the community college, experience at this level is a necessity, the primary method of gaining experience is through the intern projects in community colleges cooperating with graduate schools.

The technician in the audiovisual field has received considerable attention focused upon his duties and his training. He is a necessity within the organizational structure of the learning resources center. The technician's duties consist of the following: (1) interviews, hires and trains student assistants in the use of audiovisual equipment and location of materials; (2) operates videotape equipment and distribution of audio and video signals throughout the campus-wide closed-circuit television network and learning center; (3) schedules and supervises delivery and pick-up of equipment; and (4) prepares and reproduces instructional materials.[33]

Elwood Miller has noted that the technician must be able to communicate and work with trained professionals and therefore should have a good command of language and communications tools. His training might include (a) operation and use of equipment; (b) simple maintenance; (c) knowledge of materials services; (d) production of basic graphics for television; (e) knowledge of photography; (f) knowledge of lighting, floor direction, camera work, and prop construction; and (g) audio work necessary for production of sound tapes.[34]

In order to provide the technician with some knowledge of the educational situation in the community college, his audiovisual training should commence and terminate at the college in an audiovisual technician curriculum. Primary objectives of a program would include: an understanding of basic mass communication patterns along with electronic and engineering knowledge to support a system, an understanding of servicing audiovisual equipment, an understanding of basic production techniques, and an understanding of data processing, programmed instruction, technology, and television in order to work with others in an intelligent and productive manner.[35]

In any media program the emphasis should be centered on learning by doing and over-the-shoulder instruction. DeBernardis reports that in Portland students enrolled in media programs were given as much practical experience as possible.[36]

Summary

The success of the learning resources center in meeting the instructional objectives will depend upon the personnel and the proper administration of resources. The administrator of the center who does not consider, or is not aware of, the principles of management will have more difficulty in obtaining a cooperative and unified effort. The individual within the organization must realize his own worth to the organization and be allowed to fulfill his role.

The training of the director and library and audiovisual personnel varies considerably from institution to institution since there are not established guidelines. The director should have knowledge in both the audiovisual and library areas with additional training in curriculum supervision, administration, learning theory, and general communications. In the library area, personnel classifications are more hierarchi in nature than in the audiovisual areas, and possibly these position descriptions should be followed but not to the point that they hinde the total operation of the organization. The position of technician is somewhat ambiguous in many operating institutions and this positio is found in both the audiovisual and library areas.

The effective learning resources center will integrate these element into cohesive units. Success will come when each person realizes that he does not have a specific job but he has a responsibility, and in fulfilling this responsibility strives for excellence.

Chapter IV

FINANCE

With the diverse background and increased size of student populations, the revolutionary revisions and expansion in the curriculum, the emphasis on independent study and research, the increase in knowledge, book, and periodical production in all fields, community college libraries have had to undergo dramatic changes in their development during the past decade. The college library is no longer only a dispenser of the printed media. It must support the students, teachers, and curriculum with all types of media, including materials for independent study and programmed instruction.

To meet the need for the coordination of all forms of media for enrichment and support of the curriculum in the community college, community colleges have tended to merge the traditional library concept with the audiovisual concept to form a single theoretical unit, a learning resource center with one administrator and one budget. Consequently, this chapter will deal with a single budget which will incorporate all formats of print and nonprint media and equipment.

The business and financial administration of the college is entrusted to a number of individuals, each of whom is directly or indirectly responsible to the president. The business and financial affairs of the college are commonly delegated to a business manager whose activities include accounting, making out financial reports, cooperating in the preparation of the budget, employing non-academic personnel, supervising the physical plant, managing auxiliary enterprises, purchasing, and collecting student charges.[1]

The business manager, together with the dean of instruction and the dean of student affairs, generally make up the president's committee on the budget. In effect, it is the dean of instruction who approves or disapproves the learning resources center's budget for presentation to the president, who then presents it to the board of trustees for approval.

If the director of the center is going to successfully administer his budgeting responsibilities, he must be fully aware of the budgeting process of the institution: for instance, the time when the budget is closed for the fiscal year, when the preparation of the next year's budget must be begun, and when estimates for the fiscal year must be submitted. Since most colleges operate on a fiscal year which dates from July 1 to June 30, work on the following year's budget generally is started in November or December. In more complex situations, budget preparation often begins on next year's budget as soon as final approval is received on the current one.

The director's dealings with the dean of business or business manager generally include the following items: the placement of purchase orders, the payment of bills, the checking of the business manager's monthly accounts against the center's financial records, the inventory of equipment, the employment of nonprofessional help, the approval of major repair and renovation of the building and equipment, the transfer of funds from one budget category to another, and the approval of payroll for student employees.

Good business practices include purchasing within its prescribed budget, routing all purchase requisitions through the business office unless the director of the center is authorized to issue and sign purchase orders directly to dealers and publishers, and forwarding its bills to the business office promptly for payment. The director is expected to use his appropriation wisely and to give an exact accounting of the fund he administers. The director has the right to expect cooperation from the business manager in delegating authority to the center to purchase books, journals, and audio-visual materials and equipment, directly from dealers instead of through the business office, if this seems desirable in the local situation. With the rapid increase in enrollment, it is practically impossible to anticipate a year in advance all the items that will be needed within the fiscal year. This is particularly true of a center in the developmental stage. The cooperation of the business manager is important in assisting the center to meet unusual and unexpected financial obligations.

The center's physical plant is under the immediate direction of the superintendent of buildings and grounds, who in turn is usually directly responsible to the business manager. A good relationship with the superintendent of buildings and grounds and his staff is essential for proper maintenance and care of the physical plant.

The Budget Formulation

Budgeting is a means of planning for efficiency and economy. A budget should be planned for the present and future since it is the fiscal interpretation of the center's program. The quantity and quality of educational services supporting the curriculum are affected if some of the proposed expenditures for the fiscal year budget are reduced or eliminated. The above statement is made upon the assumption that the budget request has been prepared on the basis of actual needs, rather than with the expectation that a dollar amount reduction will be automatically applied by the administration.

Many factors are involved in the preparation of a learning resources center budget. Some of the important areas to be considered are: (1) what accrediting agency standards are involved for the institution? (2) what percentage of the total institutional budget is to be allocated for the learning resources center services? (3) is the center in the "establish*ing*" period or in the "establish*ed*" period? and (4) are funds to be allocated on a dollar basis for each department within the institution, or will the director of the center allocate purchases only when specifically requested by individual faculty and students?

There are three levels of budget planning: (1) continuity budgeting for simple continuation of an established program at its present level; (2) incremental budgeting to bring an established program up to some norm of adequacy; and (3) expansion or creative budgeting to support new goals, expanded functions, more highly developed means of implementation in an existing program or new program.[2]

Guy R. Lyle, in his book on the *Administration of the College Library,* lists six principles that should be used in budget-making:

(1)   The librarian should be invited by the president or chief budgetary officer to submit the library budget.

(2)   The budget should be submitted and approved in time for the selection and recruitment of new personnel before the next academic year begins.

(3)   The librarian should request sufficient funds in each category of the budget to support a sound program of library development.

(4)   The budget should represent library planning in terms of educational goals and not be simply a "crisis" operation in which urgent current needs are hastily converted in dollar estimates to meet a budget deadline.

(5)   The budget should be reasonably flexible in its execution.

(6)   The classification of the budget categories should enable the library to check its financial records easily.[3]

Standards established by state, regional, and national agencies and organizations have affected college libraries and their budgets

in many respects. "While, as a general rule, a college library should
receive a budget of no less than 5 percent of the total operating
budget of the college, the librarian should build a budget request
based on need. The surveyor must acquaint himself with the general
academic program of the college and its courses of instruction before
he can intelligently analyze the adequacy of the budget."[4]

Many attempts have been made by librarians and associations to
set up standards for different phases of college library work. Budgets
have been approached from the standpoint of the ratio of library
expenditures to institutional expenditures, or on a per pupil, per
faculty member, or per library staff member basis. When summarized,
these approaches show many variations in recommendations.

Any figures which are used to compare one college with another
must consider local conditions, including assessed valuation, size
of enrollment, curriculum offered, and progress stages of the different libraries.

It should be apparent that, because of the many variables which
are involved and the variations in the needs of different institutions,
no arbitrary standards will exactly fit a particular library. The
nature of the curriculum, the status of the library's holdings,
the number of personnel, the efficiency of the library organization, the physical layout of the library building or buildings, the
availability of funds, the nature of the library program, all have
to be taken into consideration in determining what the budget
of a given college library should be at a given time.[5]

The standards for Illinois junior college libraries are a good
example of the wide latitude needed to administer a state-wide
system which includes community colleges that have been in existence
for many years as an extension of the high school programs, and
those that have been established and started in the past few years
as a result of the Illinois Junior College Act of 1965. This act en-

courages that its recommendations ". . . be supplemented by the 'American Library Associations's Standards for Junior College Libraries' and by the pertinent recommendations of the North Central Association Commission on Colleges and Universities."[6] Although the ALA standards referred to above are now dated, they are reflected in the implementation carried out by other agencies.

The size of the budget inevitably determines to a large extent the scope and the effectiveness of the community college learning resources center's program. The center's holdings, the type of college it serves, the size of the faculty and student body, the variety and spread of subject fields covered, and the extent to which the college encourages the use of supplementary materials in varying formats are factors which influence budgetary needs. (See Appendix B)

The American Association of Junior Colleges, the Association of College and Research Libraries, and Association for Educational Communications and Technology have cooperatively taken a general stand in their recommendations. "Learning Resources programs budget is a function of program planning. It is designed to implement the realization of institutional and instructional program objectives."[7] The budget should reflect such factors as: the current size of the collection, the rate of growth of the institution, size of faculty, the nature of the student body, and the services to be provided.

In an assessment of Illinois community colleges, reports show that the budget of the centers varied from 1.59 percent to 12 percent of the educational fund. Some of these colleges did not have the total learning resources center budget integrated and, therefore, reported only that portion allocated to library activities. A committee of the Illinois Library Association made the following recommendations concerning budget:

(1) The ratio of the learning resource center budget to the general and educational budget should be not less than 8 percent.

(2) This percentage should begin in the third year only if the basic collection and equipment have been acquired in the first two years.[8]

As a rule of thumb, the authors of this text feel that the learning resource center budget should be approximately 6 to 10 percent of the educational fund depending upon the philosophy of the particular college and the importance it places upon the learning resources center within the college. For instance, if the college has a large television and audiovisual program, 10 percent may not cover the operating costs of the total areas under the learning resources center. The authors also feel that if the college is going to initiate audio-tutorial programs then these should be funded outside the learning resources center for if several programs are initiated in several areas during the same year, they might include at least 10 percent of the educational budget by themselves.

Administration of Budget

Administration of the budget follows approval and authorization by the college board. The authority to expend the amounts stated in the budget document should be delegated to the director of the learning resources center. As long as he expends funds within budgetary allotments, there should be no need for board approval prior to a purchase. However, the business manager of the college may require that he approve and bid certain categories of items, such as furniture and equipment.

The book fund, next to salaries, is usually the largest item in the center's budget. The monies allocated for books are usually administered in one of two ways: (1) The funds are in the hands of the director, to whom all applications are made by faculty members when they wish to order books and materials. (2) The funds are distributed in fixed amounts to the needs of each of the teaching departments. When the latter method is used, there is usually a fixed amount withheld by the librarian for reference and general subject materials, and "... consideration should be given to the systematic efforts made to supply deficiencies in the present collections."[9] Theoretically, the first plan, centralization of funds, is sound if one of two conditions exist: "(1) funds are so ample that it will seldom be necessary to deny a faculty request, or (2) funds are so small that formal apportionment is hardly worthwhile and may even discourage faculty buying."[10] Centralization of monies places a great deal of responsibility upon the director for rarely is the budget large enough to honor all requests.

Summary

At the present, the budgeting process is not always clearly defined; the techniques of formulation and execution are dependent upon the personalities involved. "The fact is that quantitative management is not used extensively in libraries at the present time. It is not difficult to find reasons for this, the basic one being that the majority of libraries are humanities-trained and oriented."[11] The learning resources center budget planning must be over a long period of time; however, awareness of the immediate needs should prevail. "It must be both short-range—today, tomorrow, and perhaps as long as the immediate year and long-range—three, five, or more years, or as far as technological and other growth factors will allow."[12]

The success of the center may depend upon the size of the budget and the manner in which it is administered. This is not to say that the learning resources center budget should be as large as the director can justify for the welfare of the various elements of the institution must be considered. Proper budget preparation and execution can make excellence a reality in the center.

Chapter V

SELECTION OF MATERIALS AND EQUIPMENT

The proper selection of materials in both print and nonprint format vitally affects the utilization of the learning resources center. Unless proper techniques and the sound judgement of the institution's personnel are utilized in the selection process, few institutions can truthfully boast of an adequate collection which meets the needs of their constituents and the educational objectives of the institution. That is to say, successful acquisition of materials is based upon the process employed and the involvement of college personnel and students.

The director of the learning resources center assumes the final responsibility for the selection process. Whereas he may not be immediately involved in the actual selection procedure, it is his responsibility to coordinate the policies of selection with the goals of the institution. For instance, if the college decides to institute new curricula in the next academic year, it is his responsibility to see that an effort is made to secure additional materials if needed. The selection of materials is influenced by the following factors: size of the institution, nature of the institution, the scope of the curriculum, the size of the current collection, the adequacy of the collection, and the funds which are currently available and the alternative modes of instruction. In the current guidelines for community college libraries "materials are selected, acquired, designed, or produced on the basis of institutional and instructional objectives, developed by the faculty, students, and administration in cooperation with Learning Resources."[1] An important factor in selection is that of the local resources of the community

and the population to be served at the college. A community college
with a large public or university library within its district or nearby
should consider sharing those resources which are of use to only an
occasional patron for there is little need to duplicate special collections.

As discussed in the opening chapter, the community college has
a wide variety of programs which it offers to a diverse population.
The community college faces the selection problems of the liberal
arts college and the vocational institution combined since it is usuall·
offering both types of curricula. At the same time, it is required
to provide materials for leisure activities and those courses offered
as non-credit adult education. The students are not those from the
upper academic level of the secondary schools of the community,
but include students of all ages and varying academic levels of performance. These are some of the general selection problems that
face the community college learning resources center in selection
of print and nonprint materials for their collections. Success will
be determined through close integration and cooperation of a united
effort by all personnel in meeting the objectives of the institution.

To promote this "working combination," there are certain components which a college will be compelled to incorporate into its
library program. Among these are: (1) a clear understanding of
what kind of library the college is supposed to be building and
for what kinds of users; (2) a genuine and general awareness of
"the different roles which different books . . . play in the intellectual life of those who come to . . . the library"; (3) an effective organization for involving the faculty and library staff in book
selection; and (4) a liberal and assured annual fund with regular
annual increases for book purchases.[2]

The criteria for selection in the audiovisual field tends to be more
teaching oriented and less collection oriented. Traditionally we have

measured the library collection in terms of books with little effort being made to assess the nonprint collection. A general statement of criteria for nonprint materials which could apply to all media is proposed by Erickson in a series of questions:

(1)   Will the materials be usable in direct relation to a teaching unit?
(2)   Is the content to be communicated by the material useful and important?
(3)   Will the material make a contribution to major teaching purposes?
(4)   Does the difficulty level of the teaching purposes (the understandings, abilities, attitudes, and appreciations) demand the help of the material being examined?
(5)   Will the material be likely to call for vicarious experiencing, thinking, reacting, discussing, studying?
(6)   Is the content to be communicated presented in terms of problems and activities of the learners?
(7)   Is the content to be presented by the material sufficiently rich in concepts and relationships?
(8)   Does the material possess appropriate content that facilitates the process of inference?
(9)   Is the material accurate, typical, and up to date?
(10) Is the kind of material uniquely adapted to the achievement of the desired teaching objective?
(11) Is the content in the material in good taste?
(12) Is the content of the material sufficiently rich in number of examples to warrant sound conclusions?[3]

Although the majority of these criteria may be applied to the selection of books as well as nonprint materials, it is hard to conceive of a librarian utilizing the entire process when selecting a volume for purchase.

In the remainder of this chapter, selection will be discussed ac-

cording to the respective areas of the learning resources center,
library and audiovisual.

Library

Criteria and Guidelines
There are many factors which determine the criteria utilized for
selection and who should participate in the selection of library
materials. The primary purpose of selection is to develop a complete
or comprehensive collection as measured by users' needs. The current
guidelines are general as they should be. They recommend that a
selection policy be developed within the institution and that all
elements of the college be involved in its development. At one time
in the history of the junior college movement, the standards were
of a quantitative nature, but this has changed to reflect criteria
based upon quality.

The adequacy of a collection cannot be measured only in
quantitative terms. "To judge a collection superior or inferior
on the basis of the volume holdings is as absurd as rating a college
on the basis of its enrollment."[4] Although the criteria have been
modified recently, the older standards enabled libraries to add
volumes with administrative support in anticipation of meeting
the regional accrediting reviews. The addition of volumes may be
harder to justify in the future.

Another technique for rating a collection is the number of books
per student. Sullivan found this criteria questionable especially for
new colleges building a foundation collection and having as yet
small enrollments. "The student or teacher in a college with 70,000
volumes probably has access to a richer and more varied array of
titles than one in a college with one-third as many, even though
the lower enrollment figure makes the ratio of books to students
seem impressively rich."[5]

Clapp and Jordan have devised another set of quantitative criteria in an attempt to measure adequacy through the operation of a formula. The factors which they consider include the following: the student body, the faculty, the curriculum, the methods of instruction, the availability of suitable places for study on the campus, the geography of the campus, and the intellectual climate.[6] This formula considers other factors than a minimum requirement for adequacy.

There are other methods of determining adequacy which are not so quantitative in nature. For instance, Lyle has suggested that the adequacy of the book collection may be measured by: (1) checking the library's holdings against standard lists; (2) checking the library's holdings against selective lists; (3) assessing the book collection in terms of utilization; (4) the ratio of success to failure in efforts to secure books; and (5) the expenditures for library materials compared with data from other institutions.[7]

The criteria for determining an adequate collection is still debatable. At the present, the guidelines do not suggest a minimum number of volumes as a foundation for a community college collection. The adequacy of the collection is ultimately determined by the utilization of the faculty and students.

Problems in Building a Collection

Who is responsible for selecting books in the community college? As one might expect, the answer usually varies from institution to institution. In some community colleges the library staff will play a major role and in others the faculty will assume this role. In most cases students are allowed to select material; however, when compared to the total requests student selection is almost insignificant.

The trend in academic libraries has been toward selection by library personnel rather than selection by faculty.

A survey of the literature of book selection in academic libraries

indicates that there has been for more than a half-century a continuing shift from faculty-dominated selection to library-dominated
selection. It appears likely that the trend will continue, because
of the increased use of subject specialists on library staffs, the
growth of the publication industry, the articulation of more selection policy statements, as well as increasingly widespread
recognition of selection as part of the librarian's professional
responsibility.[8]

Lane also notes that faculty-library cooperation is more wide-
spread in smaller libraries. He makes the following note in reference
to Canadian libraries: "Book selection should be the joint responsibility of the teaching staff and the library staff. The teaching staff
should be consulted about the books needed for the present and
future teaching programs . . . within the defined policy for the collection."[9]

James Schmidt, however, points out that those assuming selection
responsibilities are often determined by the budget allocation.
"Whether the library staff or the faculty has the primary responsibility for selection materials seems to hinge on whether or not the
[book] budget is allocated to instructional units."[10]

The question of professionalism plays a major role in determining the selection procedures. Librarians look upon selection as a
professional responsibility rather than a task to be delegated or
shifted to other entities. But for the faculty to utilize a collection
to its maximum, it is necessary that they feel as if they have a
personal interest in the facility and perhaps by closely involving
them in selection they will feel the responsibility to encourage and
require its use. Branscomb notes that certain questions will call
for leadership and guidance on the librarian's part. They would
include: "(1) Should the library buy textbooks? (2) Should the
library purchase rare books or collector's items? (3) Should the
college library purchase fiction and items related to any course of

instruction? (4) Should the college purchase research material? and (5) What can be done to improve the quality of book selections in departmental fields?"[11] Haro points out that ". . . while most academic librarians now agree that they [librarians] should engage in book selection, there is at present little agreement on selection methods and procedures."[12]

In a recent study, de los Santos studied the effects of certain factors on the book collections in Texas junior colleges. He divided the libraries into high-index and low-index categories according to book-use, per-student library expenditure, library holdings and percent of instruction budget allocated to the library. He found that librarians in high-index libraries (1) spent more time in book selection, (2) made more use of selection aids, (3) were better prepared professionally, and (4) had more library work experience.[13]

Bach notes a strong concern about the librarian, professionalism, and selection.

> It is the writer's conviction that the librarian ought to assume responsibility for the development of the library collection. If a librarian fails to act the part of a librarian, what is he? He is a custodian of books, a glorified research assistant, a business manager at the most. . . . Librarians ought to consult with the faculty, librarians ought to take advantage of the special advice that is available to them, but librarians ought not to depend on the faculty to do three jobs—teach, do research and develop library collections. It is unfair to the faculty and it is unfair to the library.[14]

Selection in the community college cannot be an either-or proposition. The responsibility is shared since in most instances the librarians are not competent in all subject matter areas and each faculty member does not understand the total collection development. The success of the cooperation of librarians and faculty in selection will be reflected later in utilization patterns by students and faculty. That is to say, faculty involvement on the community college campus in book selection is a must.

One of the major problems facing the learning resources center is the development of the collection concerned with vocational education. Since the vocational area is a major element of the total curricula, certain allotments should be made in the library collection. "The selection of technical and vocational materials for junior colleges may be classified as a problem. In a sense, this dilemma is something like that of the weather in that everybody talks about it, but nobody does anything about it."[15] The authors of the quotation above have also listed three major factors which contribute to the problem: (1) the number and variety of technical-vocational programs, (2) the orientation of the junior college librarian, and (3) the lack of published selection guides. Commenting upon library personnel and vocational education, these authors note the following:

> Selection is further complicated by the nontechnical orientation of many junior college librarians. They often hold undergraduate degrees in the humanities, rather than the sciences and so may lack the scientific and technical background which would enhance their selection capabilities. As junior colleges expand and new institutions are opened, librarians are drawn from other areas of the profession such as the high school, the public library, and the four-year college library. This sets the stage for a period of re-education and experimentation before the junior college librarian can meaningfully begin his selection tasks.[16]

John Harvey, commenting upon this problem, has stated that ". . . in a terminal program the practical arts will be emphasized and a more technical book collection required, perhaps even a better technical book collection than is found in the four-year college.[17]

The selection of materials of a controversial nature is a difficult problem for some institutions due to factors such as the community, the administration, the board, the student body, and librarians themselves. The position stated in the guidelines is as follows: "Learning Resources Programs provide materials presenting all sides of controversial issues. The position of the American Library Association, and comparable associations, on the subject of censorship is firmly adhered to."[18]

The Library Bill of Rights notes that materials "selected should be chosen for values of interest, information and enlightenment of all people of the community. In no case should library materials be excluded because of the race or nationality or the social, political, or religious views of the authors. Libraries should provide books and other materials presenting all points of view concerning the problems and issues of our time . . ."[19]

Although these censorship positions are clear on the stand that librarians should take, the director would be well advised to make the president of the college aware of these policies and perhaps even obtain approval of the policy from the college board for at some point in time the question of censorship will arise. "Most persons agree that the library should provide material on all sides of controversial questions, but the application of this principle to specific cases is often difficult. How many and what books should the library have in favor of communism? If a local Birch Society presents the library with twenty-five books on the far right, should the library accept them and then proceed to balance them with an equal number on the far left?"[20]

The Collection

As has been previously pointed out, the collections will and should vary considerably due to the nature of the institution. In a

questionnaire sent to the subscribers of *Choice*, it was found that
of 263 junior colleges responding, "two hundred and fifteen had
collections of up to and including 25,000 volumes; thirty-six had
between 25,000 and 50,000; eleven had from 50,000 to 100,000;
and one had a collection of 500,000 volumes."[21] In the same report, the mean of the total collections was composed of 36.1 percent humanities, 34.6 percent social sciences, 6.9 percent natural
science and mathematics, 7.4 percent bio-medical, 5.0 percent
engineering, and 5.3 percent unclassified. The current acquisitions
included 34.1 percent humanities, 34.2 percent social science,
6.9 percent natural sciences and mathematics, 7.5 percent bio-
medical, 6.0 percent engineering, and 7.4 percent as unclassified.[22]

Peggy Sullivan found that the number of subscriptions to periodicals varied from fewer than 100 to more than 1,000 selections.[23]
In an early study, Bensen concluded that "more than half of the
use of periodicals seems to have been more or less unrelated to
course work."[24] If this still holds true, increased attention should
be given to the acquisition of magazines for recreational reading.

The selection of materials varies from institution to institution
as does the size of the collection. That is, there are no set criteria
or models for an institution to follow in terms of acquisition of
materials, and each should select according to the objectives of the
institution for developing a quality collection.

Selection Aids

Currently there are several selection aids to help the community
college librarian begin or strengthen an existing collection. Perhaps
none has received the attention which the "Opening Day Collection"
of *Choice* has received. This collection of 1,716 volumes has been
used primarily as a guideline for a beginning collection; however,
most community colleges should have a large percentage of the
titles. *Choice* is a monthly periodical, started in March 1964, and
contains reviews of academic books written by subject specialists.

Other selection aids particularly useful at the two-year college level are *Books for College Libraries, Books for Junior Colleges, The Junior College Library Collection, A Basic Book Collection for the Community College,* and *The Vocational Technical Library Collection.* In addition to these tools, the general selection tools useful for all types of libraries should not be overlooked. Periodicals such as *Publishers' Weekly, Library Journal,* and New York Times *Book Review* and annuals such as *Books in Print* and *Reader's Advisor* are invaluable.

Commercial sources of information such as publishers' catalogs and selection plans should be approached with caution but never disregarded. None of the reviewing sources or selection lists can cover the masses of new material appearing on the market each year. Consequently, many useful and needed titles are only brought to the librarian's attention through sales catalogs and circulars or the selection plans of book jobbers. In addition, teachers' requests for new materials are most often prompted by such sources. The selection policy and criteria must be carefully and conscientiously applied to titles selected in this manner, and in most cases, the most important factor is the experienced person. One such plan sends facsimile catalog cards of titles recently published and suitable for college and university collections to subscribing libraries. The subscribing library simply selects those titles which they wish to acquire and returns these facsimile cards to the jobber, thus eliminating at least one step in the selection procedure and perhaps several in the ordering process.

The selection process in a community college learning resources center is a complex task involving faculty, students, and librarians. Selection policy needs to be formulated for each institution and examined periodically to see if the center is moving in the desired direction. The quality of the collection should be measured by the degree to which it fulfills the needs of the institution.

Audiovisual

The selection procedure for audiovisual materials does not appear to have as many ramifications as for print media. For instance nonprint materials are not usually purchased in as great a volume as print materials, and the selection policies for print media also apply to non print materials. However, nonprint media selection suffers from a lack of basic unified quantitative standards and ambiguous definitions of personnel roles. This is not to indicate that nonprint materials are less important in the teaching effort, but rather selection policies in each field have evolved differently and separately. If a unified center is maintained, there should be an integrated selection policy covering all media. It will be the purpose of this section to explore the selection of audiovisual materials and equipment.

Materials

The selection of nonprint materials has traditionally been the responsibility of the instructor working through proper audio-visual personnel. Very few instances have been found in which the audiovisual specialist had the exclusive role in selection of nonprint materials. The selection of audiovisual materials traditionally has been more teaching oriented than has been the selection of library books. Audiovisual personnel are generally more knowledgeable about learning theory and nonverbal communication than librarians. Thus the impact of a book upon the individual has not been considered in the same frame of reference as the impact of audiovisual materials. Books are traditionally worthy, but nonprint media still requires justification. In the community college budget considerably more money is usually budgeted for books than for prepared audiovisual materials. "Too frequently instructional materials selection has been based on the desires of the teacher and not the needs of the learner. The key curriculum issues appear to be: (a) need for establishing priority, (b) importance of learning how to learn, (c) need to see the school program as a totality, and (d) caution in promotion of easy to adopt packaged programs."[25] How many books are selected without considering the above factors?

The production or selection of nonprint materials is developed upon an instructional design. Attention is devoted to the learner, the subject content, the process of learning, and other factors influencing the learning process.

The design requires this sequence of activities:

(1) Set objectives in terms of the individual's needs in a changing society.
(2) Select subject content to serve the objectives.
(3) Develop learning experiences in terms of the most efficient and effective instructional methods, keeping in mind the requirements and limitations of budget, personnel, facilities, equipment, and schedules.
(4) Select and prepare instructional materials that fit the learning experiences and methods.
(5) Test the materials with a sampling of learners.
(6) Revise materials as necessary to satisfy the objectives.
(7) Carry out the instruction.
(8) Evaluate the results and revise elements in the design, as necessary, for future uses.[26]

The actual criteria for the selection of a particular nonprint item should include the following items: (1) the material reflects sound scholarship and retains the vitality of the original ideas; (2) the material covers the topic or topics as intensively and extensively as the teacher feels is appropriate for the class; (3) the total material selected for the course fulfills the objectives for the course; (4) the material selected is organized in a manner that enhances the development considered central for the course; and (5) the total material selected for a given course reflects an awareness of the range of

individual differences that will be present in the given class.[27]
The criteria of *technical* excellence is also vitally important in
selection. This may not be the case in book selection. Erickson
has proposed a list of relationships that will determine whether
the materials are of acceptable quality. Questions to be asked are:

1. Is technical quality of the material artistic?
2. Is the producer's mode of communication adequate for the
   purpose? That is, is the message put over clearly, forcefully,
   in ways that attract and hold attention?
3. Are physical size, format, and color satisfactory?
4. Is workmanship in the construction of the material adequate?
5. Is the content to be presented free of conflicts and distrac-
   tions?
6. Was careful planning by the producer obvious in the content
   structure of the material?
7. Did the producer of the material set out to produce the
   material for school audiences with competent educational
   consultants?[28]

Erickson further indicates that "teachers should base their selection of high quality audiovisual materials upon valid teaching purposes (objectives) and upon the unique characteristics of a specific
group of learners."[29]

The emphasis on technical quality is necessarily more pronounced
for nonprint materials selection than for print materials. The most
obvious difference, however, as has been previously mentioned, is
the tendency to purchase nonprint materials only when needed for
a specific teaching circumstance. The available criteria for nonprint
materials is definitely cued to the teacher's instructional efforts
rather than the students' independently motivated efforts to learn.
If we are to have a truly unified and integrated collection of materials
to meet the needs of all center users, then nonprint materials must

be selected and purchased in the same manner as print items. The center must make its commitment to a balanced collection in terms of content and user needs rather than in terms of format. To restrict the acquisition of nonprint materials to the needs presented by specific classroom circumstances only is to deny many students the means to capitalize upon their own learning requirements as well as to deny access to a widely varied and rich source of information.

Selection Aids

The development of a well balanced collection of media complementing the curricula is not usually considered within the total learning resources center. More specifically, as noted above, consideration is usually given to purchase of materials for a given set of circumstances rather than for balance in the total collection. Locating materials and equipment which meet the specified objectives is a problem.

The National Information Center for Educational Media has published several indexes covering various formats. They include the following: *Index to 16mm Educational Films, Index to 35mm Filmstrips, Index to Educational Audio Tapes, Index to Educational Video Tapes, Index to Educational Records, Index to 8mm Cartridges, Index to Producers and Distributors, Index to Black History and Studies, Index to Educational Overhead Transparencies.* The *Great Plains Video Tape Catalog* and the *National Audio Tape Catalogue* along with professional magazines in the field are helpful guides.

Although selection of equipment varies among institutions, one aid which will assist in selection is the *Audio-Visual Equipment Directory* published by the National Audio-Visual Association. This volume is annually revised, and it contains the specifications, suggested list price, and a photograph of most of the equipment currently manufactured.

"It would appear that the problems of locating materials fade in their significance when compared to the problems inherent in an adequate evaluation."[30]

Selection of Equipment

The nature and amount of equipment will influence the success of the entire media program. The director should be kept informed for his approval will usually be needed before equipment is bid or directly purchased. The equipment to be purchased should be evaluated in terms of the designated objectives for the instructional package. Erickson reports there are two important aspects to general selection of audiovisual equipment: (1) the process of selection, and (2) the standardization of equipment brands.[31]

The process of selection in the community college usually is handled within the learning resources center. However, when more extensive items are considered such as a television studio, a language laboratory, or a dial retrieval installation, a committee may prove helpful in terms of support and justification. It is recommended that one committee member be from the business office staff to assist in better planning for such large expenditures.

Standardization

In some instances, there will be pressure not to standardize, but the advantages outweigh the disadvantages:

(1)   It is easier to train teachers and students to operate the equipment; hence less time and effort will be spent by supervisory personnel on this phase of service.

(2)   There will be fewer operational failures in the classroom because more people will understand how to control the output of the equipment.

(3)   It is easier to service one make of machine because local servicemen are more familiar with it and understand how to fix or adjust it.

(4)   It is cheaper to service the equipment since only one set
      of spare parts needs to be maintained. Therefore, less
      money needs to be tied up in a stock of spare parts during
      any one year.
(5)   There is less clerical and technical work involved in main-
      taining the inventory of spare parts, and in storing, organiz-
      ing, and finding space for them.
(6)   Standardization under school-system policy eliminates
      wrangling with distributors every time an order is sent
      out for bids.[33]

The general criteria for selection can be comprised of the following: (1) portability, (2) ruggedness, (3) cost, (4) ease of operation,
(5) quality of performance, (6) effective design, (7) ease of maintenance and repair, (8) reputation of the manufacturer, (9) local equipment status, and (10) available service.[34]

Summary

The selection of materials and equipment for the learning resources
center is a vital element in meeting the needs of students and faculty.
Selection procedures are based primarily upon meeting the instructional objectives of the college. Establishment of guidelines noting
general procedures and trends to follow in selection is a necessity.
Such guidelines should be examined regularly and modified as the
need arises.

The selection of materials and equipment has local priority and
standard guidelines cannot be utilized in total. Influencing factors
of the institute may include its nature, its curriculum, its budget,
and its size and adequacy of the existing collection. When establishing a collection the emphasis should be upon the total concept of
materials in print and nonprint formats.

Adequacy will be measured according to the combination of
materials in an integrated and unified fashion and the success of

the center will depend upon how well the selection process has been accomplished throughout the history of the institution. An excellent collection does not just happen by chance.

Chapter VI

INSTRUCTIONAL AND TECHNICAL SERVICES

The services of the learning resources center should be directed toward the users: faculty, students, and the community. The multitude of services provided can and will be categorized into two major headings—instructional and technical. The discussion of instructional services will include the philosophy of utilization and studies of actual utilization in both community and four-year colleges. The discussion of technical services will concern itself largely with acquisition and processing the materials for use. A close relationship and sense of understanding between both services is necessary. Technical services are essential and must be integrated into the philosophy of instructional service if the center is to provide excellence of service to its users. Tauber has noted a trend to break up technical services into smaller units in the university, and he states, "Despite this general pattern, there exists an administrative organization which groups the various services into two major units—the technical services and the reader's services."[1]

Instructional Services

In general, instructional services may be designated as reader's services; however, reader's services will be integrated into the whole and not treated as a specific entity in this discussion. Two areas of instructional services will be discussed: the philosophy of service, and the actual research which has been conducted upon utilization of the facility.

Philosophy of Service

When analyzing the philosophy of service of the learning resources center, one must ask the questions: To whom will the
service be given; and, what will be the nature of the services?

Since the community college is comprised of, and supported by,
its district, it should be assumed that service will be provided for
all citizens of the community college district. Administrators are
always reminding the citizens that it is the citizens' college. If
community support is desired, facilities, including the learning
resources center, should be open to community use. If citizens are
to have access to community college materials all libraries of the
district need to be integrated in a unified network, thus allowing
a sharing of all facilities to all persons.

In a survey Josey reports that most two-year colleges permit
some degree of access to their library collections and resources,
but further states that "by and large, most of the two-year institutions have not formulated policy statements which govern the use
of their libraries by outsiders."[2]

A more pressing problem is how available services are "sold,"
especially to the enrolled students and faculty. Research indicates
that the most effective approach to students is through the faculty.

> The contention that teachers do not promote the use of the
> library is a gross understatement. It appears, rather, that
> teachers discourage rather than encourage the use of library
> resources.
>
> Many or perhaps most college students never discover the
> attributes of the library because they are able to complete their
> courses by following a debilitating plan. Course outlines are
> accompanied by bibliographies which, despite the variations in
> manner of citation, generally manage to indicate not only the
> exact volume, but the precise pages which the student is ex-
> pected to consult.[3]

The librarian can to some degree offset this rigid tendency. The involvement of the student and faculty in an inquiry process in which each user is the initiator and accepts the responsibility for the final outcome is the aim of the librarian. Sister Sheehan has successfully described the purpose of the center in the following passage.

> We want to reverse the process, to change the emphasis so that the student will be the prime mover in his own education. We want him to dig for himself in the realms of gold, to sift and weigh what he finds, and to treasure, not a miscellany of facts, but the joy and the challenge of discovery, of straining to penetrate deeper and deeper into the world of knowledge. And by knowledge, we don't mean facts. It is abundantly evident that most of today's facts will be obsolescent data in ten years. By knowledge in this context, we mean appreciation of beauty in all its forms and the ability, by inductive or deductive reasoning, to assemble from contemporary data an intellectual structure adequate to the contemporary world.[4]

In order to achieve such a goal, libraries are going to have to change their techniques and processes. For instance, Sheehan asks the following questions: Is book-selection subject-centered or student-centered? Do we capitalize on students' current interests and enthusiasms? Are current periodicals available for student reading? Have we broadened our orientation program beyond the freshman level? Do students use libraries as they would like to, or as we force them to? Do we welcome student suggestions? Do we make the collection as accessible as possible? "In short, is our library planned for students? If not, why are we in business?"[5]

The same questions are applicable to the learning resources center as a whole, not only to the library segment. The practical need for the use of all resources will have to be illustrated by faculty and center personnel working in harmony together to serve the student. Both software and hardware should be available for student utilization. Is not the production of an 8mm film on a certain concept as important as a creatively written composition? "In the final analysis it is the richness of a library center and its efficiency in servicing what it owns that reflects excellence or lack of it. About that it is the users who know most."[6]

In order to assess further implications of future and effective planning and organization, we must study the state of the art as it now exists. Only then can we make the needed changes.

Research on Student Utilization

Four studies have provided an in-depth analysis of students' use of the library at both two-year and four-year institutions. Studies by Hostrop and Allen pertained to the community college, while the Knapp and Clayton studies dealt with students in small four-year institutions.

Hostrop, while investigating students at the College of the Desert, California, found the following characteristics connected with library utilization.

(1) Junior college students use the library facilities for course purposes less than twenty-three per cent of their in-use time. The in-use was chiefly as a study hall.

(2) Reserve loans amounted to less than twelve per cent.

(3) Junior college students borrowed from the general collection at a rate of 18.96 loans for the academic year.

(4) Full-time students borrowed considerably more than did part-time students.

(5) Twenty-five per cent of the courses accounted for 95.49 per cent of the total loans.

(6) Library-impelling instructors shared common characteristics which included explicit assignments, provisions of

specific titles or bibliographies, continual follow-up on library assignments, requirement that sources be cited in student papers, insistence upon high standards, and expression of their own fondness for books.

(7) Students who were heavy borrowers fell into two main categories: they used library materials either because of course demands, usually term papers, or because they had a personal fondness for books.

(8) Nearly ninety per cent of all graded classes were found to be library independent.

(9) The library user had the following characteristics: female; living at home; better scholarship; worked half-hour less for pay during each week; higher socio-economic stratum and had more books in home; and enrolled in courses in art history, English and speech, introduction to music, electronic circuitry, health, physical education, recreation, geology, history, philosophy, government, sociology, religion, and general psychology.

The non-user more likely had the following characteristics: male; living away from home; lower scholarship; completed more units of work; worked one-half hour more per-week; lower socio-economic stratum; enrolled in courses in agriculture, business, engineering, fire science, foreign languages, mathematics and police science.[7]

Allen reported a study comprised of approximately 6,000 questionnaires at three community colleges during the fall of 1969. The study consisted of questionnaires to study student attitudes, faculty attitudes, and to measure the actual use of materials while in the library by both students and faculty. A summary of the hypotheses of this study follows:

(1) Sophomore students did not have more favorable attitudes

and utilization patterns than freshmen, but freshmen and
sophomore students had more favorable attitudes and
utilization patterns than unclassified students;

(2)   Full-time students depended upon the library more than
part-time students, and they had more favorable attitudes
and utilization patterns. In many cases, use of the community
college library was not important to part-time students as
reflected by their statements;

(3)   Students enrolled in transfer, general studies, and occupational curricula had similar attitudes and utilization patterns;
they varied greatly from the unclassified students;

(4)   The levels of educational development among faculty members had little importance in reflecting attitudes or in mani-
festing utilization patterns;

(5)   Faculty members teaching in the humanities division did
not have more favorable attitudes and utilization patterns
than faculty members teaching in other divisions.[8]

Howard Clayton, at a small four-year institution, investigated
whether socio-economic backgrounds of students played a significant role in library utilization. He found that the mean number of
loans per year was 15.47 volumes and that occupation and education of the parents had little effect upon student use. Pupils from
institutions with under 850 enrollment borrowed more reserve books
than those over 850; students from families with incomes of less
than $4,000 borrowed more books than did pupils whose families
earned over $16,000; and students in the lower quartile made little
use of the library.[9]

In a notable study at Knox College, a four-year liberal arts institution, Knapp reported the following results:

(1)   Less than twenty per cent of the students accounted for
more than half of the borrowing. Less than half of the

students accounted for about 90 per cent of the borrowing.

(2) One-fourth of the courses accounted for almost 90 per cent of total circulation.

(3) Detailed examination of individual library-dependent courses, and of certain others, revealed considerable variety in teaching methods and student borrowing.

(4) Small advance classes were the only classes to stimulate extensive and/or problem-solving use of the library.[10]

Knapp in a later report of the same study indicated:

Neither subject field, nor teaching method, nor kind of assignment, nor quality of students in a class is of crucial importance in determining whether or not a given course will be dependent upon the library. The only decisive factor seems to be—and this is a subjective judgment—the instructor's attitude. Almost invariably students used the library less than the instructor expected them to. The evidence presented there indicates that the college library is not the heart of the college. Students read what they have to read.[11]

Harvie Branscomb in *Teaching With Books* noted ". . . the existence of a large percentage of undergraduates who make such slight use of the college library that they would scarcely miss it if it ceased to exist."[12]

Clark, analyzing community college students at Wright Campus of Chicago City College, found that of 729 students (27.3 percent of the borrowers) accounted for 729 (5.6 percent) of the circulations. At the other extreme, eighteen borrowers (0.67 percent) accounted for 724 circulations. The better students were found to be heavier users than the average borrowers. However, the heaviest library users were not the best students.[13]

A survey at El Camino College indicated that approximately 90

percent of the students in the library were using the facility as a
study hall. In this self-study, the students reported that instructors
encourage effective use of the library by making assignments in
library materials, by suggesting books for supplementary material,
and by telling their classes about interesting material. Faculty
members reported they used the library by assigning and suggesting the use of library materials, by placing books on reserve, by
"keeping up" with materials in their fields and by taking classes
to the library to show them materials for use in their courses. The
students reported that the teachers might improve by making
additional assignments.[14]

The studies and statements noted have a strong connection with
library utilization in the community college library. There are
many additional user studies pertaining to the four-year universities.

Gorham Lane reviewed four studies which were conducted over
a period of two years. One analysis of the sample by school and
class showed that fewer than 30 percent of the total number of
students in the school were using the library facilities. The library
was regarded as a place for study and required reading, and the use
of the library for this purpose increased year by year from freshman through senior year. Further analysis indicated that approximately 4 percent of the freshmen in the library were using library
materials only; the comparable figure for seniors was 19 percent.[15]

Behling and Cudd designed a questionnaire to determine the
ways in which users avail themselves of the facilities, the characteristics of library users, the users' opinions of the library and its
services. The results indicated the following: 55 percent were using
the library only for study purposes; this group was more dissatisfied
than those seeking service or information; history majors and
faculty were the heaviest users, followed by students in education,
business, political science, and English, and that the questionnaire
was effective for measurement of library-campus relations.[16]

Jain reported in a study conducted at Purdue University during the summer of 1964 that 60 percent of library patrons used their own material, 54 percent used library material, and 20 percent checked out material for home use. On the average a library patron spent two hours and twelve minutes in the library and used three titles during the visit.[17]

Only a sample of the multitude of user studies available has been presented here. The data indicates that most students use the library to study their own materials thus supporting the accusation that the library serves as a study hall for the majority of students. Since the community college consists largely of commuting students, this concept is reinforced. The resources of the library are not fully utilized and to date student use of the audiovisual facilities of the learning resources center is practically non-existent as measured by published research, especially within the community college.

Technical Services

As noted above, effective utilization of the learning resources center is difficult to obtain on the community college campus. The students are not required to use the materials and in some cases do not know what resources in print and nonprint formats are available to them. "Materials should be organized and classified to enable the student to get an over-all view of the things he can utilize. Such an effort must be indicated by the community college administrators. Our group stressed again that our goal is to prepare a student for a lifetime of study. What do we do to get the student into the library? How does one convey the value of the library?"[18]

One of the major concepts presented here is the need for unification of all materials. This particularly applies to the card catalog. A user must have easy access to both the materials and the interfiled catalog. The technical services department in most community colleges handles the work of cataloging, classification, and physical preparation, as well as ordering and the bookkeeping function (in order to keep a check on the budget when materials are ordered). The work area for technical services should be organized to allow a work flow beginning with ordering and ending with the finished product ready for the shelves. General cataloging and the classification function, and the role of automation in assisting technical services, will be considered below.

Classification

One of the first decisions that a director of the learning resources center will have to make concerns the classification scheme: Dewey or Library of Congress. Rowland in a survey approximately ten years ago reported that of 336 replies, 96.5 percent used the Dewey Decimal Classification scheme and only 3.5 percent used the Library of Congress. He further states, "It would seem that whether the library is a junior college or 4-year institution, Dewey is the prevalent scheme for small collections."[19] Peggy Sullivan reporting later statistics indicates that of fifty-two institutions, thirty-one used Dewey, ten the Library of Congress, and eleven were converting to Library of Congress from Dewey Decimal. "As stated, the statistics indicate a strong trend toward newer institutions adopting LC initially and of older ones converting to it when feasible."[20] Some of the general reasons for using the Library of Congress classification are: it covers a constantly expanding universe of knowledge without signs of cracking at the seams; it was not designed to be logical therefore the catalogers have to use the guides or wait for cards when classifying; it is diffused; its growth is not hindered by its notation; its class numbers are printed on almost all Library of Congress cards; and it presents no overpowering problems for automation. One disadvantage is that it is difficult for the browser to use. "It has tremendous potential for adaptation, growth, expansion, and change. It is wide open in an age of logical dead ends and leaping cross fertilization. The limits of its future extension are bounded only by human imagination."[21]

No single system is used currently in the classification of nonprint media. "People have developed systems for various media but no single system has been developed that will meet the needs in all situations for all media."[22] In 1968, the Department of Audiovisual Instruction (Association for Educational Communications and Technology) issued a document concerned with what elements should be incorporated into the catalog descriptions of audiovisual media and how such catalogs should be arranged. These guidelines suggest consideration of the following factors: (1) title, (2) type of medium, (3) physical description, (4) maturity range, (5) content description, (6) year, (7) producer-sponsor-distributor, (8) subject headings, (9) classification numbers, and (10) format.[23] Louis Brown, in 1969, recommended the use of the Library of Congress system because of the following characteristics: (1) it organizes media material consistently according to content areas; (2) one can provide a computer printout using the broad headings or detailed subheadings; (3) it allows an integration with the print media; (4) it allows consistent classification; (5) it allows readily accessible printouts with additional information; and (6) it allows a complete breakdown of specific content areas enabling libraries to use computerized bookings and to substitute titles if the requested ones are not available.[24] Quinly had noted earlier that "for several years the Library of Congress has been issuing catalog cards on films and filmstrips, but through a lack of communication on the part of audiovisual directors and the absence of complete cooperation from the film producers, the catalog cards are not widely accepted."[25]

In classification of records, where obviously "the classification scheme in a collection of five thousand albums is likely to be far more complex than that used in a collection of five hundred albums"[26] and particularly if the collection is open to patrons, the same arrangement as used for library books and other materials is most appropriate. Thus the choice of the best possible classification scheme is important, but just as important is the use of the one scheme to classify all media materials.

Cataloging

The divided catalog (i.e. the filing of author and title cards together, with the subject headings in a separate file) is currently being used in many community college learning resource centers. "Size itself, is not considered a handicap by librarians shifting to the divided catalog. Librarians who have divided their catalogs believe that the change has helped users and reduced problems in filing."[27] The authors agree with the concept of the divided catalog for community college libraries.

The book catalog (as opposed to the card catalog) has received attention in many districts with more than one campus since several catalogs are needed and the collections are usually quite similar. Not only do the costs of production vary considerably in relationship to the quality of the end product, but other variables to be considered are: the collection to be catalogued, the finished product, and the characteristics of the production method.[28]

The procedures used in community college learning resources centers are different for each institution when it comes to cataloging and classification.

> The simple truth is that methods of processing in a more or less homogeneous group of libraries are so bewildering in their variety and ingenious in their meeting of problems in different ways that any attempt to capture a true picture of them on paper produces results that must be approached cautiously. . . . Junior college libraries are different now from what they were ten years ago: larger, more completely oriented to the college field, and more in tune with current professional thought. The next ten years will without doubt see similar changes.[29]

Automation

Automation in the media field is receiving increased attention due to the following factors: we are living in a technological society; the increasing costs of service; the emphasis upon professional personnel doing professional duties; and the inadequate supply of trained professionals and support personnel in the area of media services. As new and efficient solutions to these problems are contemplated, the computer and automated devices will be relied upon to relieve the employee for additional service to students and faculty. "Effective use of the library has been demanded by the educational system, for elementary and secondary schools as well as institutions of higher learning. In recent years the introduction of automation into a variety of learning and teaching activities has provided the librarian with potentially powerful tools for increasing his effectiveness as a communicator, though the capabilities of these developments have not yet been fully realized."[30]

Although automation is somewhat new to media service, personnel have envisioned it either as a nightmare, or, on the other hand, as a tireless ingenious machine. Automation is but a means to accomplish a particular goal of better service to users more effectively and efficiently. The machine is not the mind of the human, and it cannot perform the tasks of identifying values or dealing with the complexity of human leadership and understanding. The machine, however, can perform accurate statistical counts, and thereby release personnel to perform more professional roles.

Both library and audiovisual personnel in the learning resources center have a responsibility to become informed about the changes which automation can bring to service. The personnel will fill the roles of communicator, advisor, and planner in promoting change; it is their duty to serve as the liaison, and through their specialized knowledge, help plan the learning resources center's system.

Allen Veaner points out that automation can do "formalizable, housekeeping work. Hence the candidates for automation are of two kinds: repetitive tasks and those jobs which are deterministic and highly structured. They must involve relatively few intellectual decisions or decisions which are both repetitive and comparatively low order."[31]

How can automation assist services such as circulation, technical processes, acquisitions, and serials? It is not the purpose of this discussion to review specific automated equipment, but rather to review applications.

In large community colleges circulation control is one of the most costly services to be performed. The systems for control vary as do the nature of the centers. For instance, the "off-line" or "batch-processing" methods may meet the needs of most centers, but for some this may be too slow and an "on-line" or "real-time" system is needed. The circulation system can be constructed so that a minimum of personal contact is necessary. Data collection for both charging and discharging and for the printing of overdue notices can be efficiently conducted without manual intervention.

The automated system can perform the following tasks in acquisitions: prepare orders sent to booksellers, keep record of all current outstanding orders, prepare reminders, handle accounting procedures processs accessions, and provide processing slips which accompany the book to cataloging. This form of automation can liberate the staff from nonproductive and repetitive tasks such as alphabetizing and recopying of bibliographic information.

Perhaps the majority of articles produced on automation within the last decade have dealt with the book catalog and/or the cataloging process. The primary task is the creation of a multiplicity of entries in various forms and from one catalog record. This record can produce sets of catalog cards in duplicate or print book-form catalogs for distribution to all branches. Computer programs are being used to file the completed cards in the proper sequence. In an article about MARC (machine readable cataloging), Avram discusses the pilot project and what MARC might do for cataloging standardization of bibliographic information.[32] Through this pilot project and the later MARC II project, flexibility of records in machine readable form has been facilitated. The impact the MARC project will have upon community colleges at this time is unknown.

A printed list of periodical holdings for one or for a number of locations on campus is not too difficult a task. However, when one attempts to produce automatically periodical binding lists, claims, and arrivals, some problems occur. A computer-produced serials list can be produced in sufficient numbers to be distributed to other campus locations, and such lists are easier and more convenient to use. Full automation of the tasks mentioned is very attractive because of the saving in time spent on clerical tasks. However, the exceptions in periodicals—such as the frequency of issues—can present difficult problems. For instance, Miami-Dade Community College has been utilizing a similar system. "The major problems were conceded to be: keeping abreast of claims; maintaining accurate. readable, up-to-date inventory files which would indicate whether the item was bound, unbound, or in microform; binding control which wou indicate color code, relevant information about the index, date sent to binder, and cost."[33]

A word of caution is necessary. To quote Parker, "Data processing is not a plaything. In a number of libraries I know, the approaches to data processing have been little more than this . . . the record to be created by data processing must replace another record if it is to be economically advantageous. A supplementary record can only add to the total cost, and it will probably not be kept up-to-date after the novelty wears off."[34]

However, the success of automation in networks and cooperative sharing is described by Beaker: "A library communications network utilizing many of the ideas described here may bring us a wholly new approach to library service. An approach in which librarians will increasingly share their resources with one another rather than concentrate in developing competitive collections. But technology alone is not enough."[35]

The EDUCOM alliance may provide further utilization.

All information-processing facets are of concern to the alliance; for example, computerized programmed instruction, library automation, educational television and radio, and the use of computers in university administration and in clinical practice. A major contention of the council is that multimedia computerized networks ultimately must connect campuses across the continent. These electronic links will permit the instant sharing of audiovisual and other resources of books, documents, research results, and even the time of professors.[36]

The present state of library automation is diverse. There are discrepancies between the theoretical, as written in journals, and the practical, as actually operating in the field. In order to efficiently operate and develop automation, community colleges need to assess their needs and develop applications for their own situation. Effective use of automation in media activities assumes increased regional and system cooperation in producing software and in maintaining the expensive hardware. (Computer services are also discussed in Chapter 9.)

By releasing professional personnel from repetitive tasks, automation can help to meet the needs of users. However, first the professional personnel needs to learn and to understand the various applications possible; only then will effective automation become a reality.

Summary

In the community college effective service depends upon the utilization of the learning resources center by faculty and students. The published studies of utilization in four-year and community colleges indicate that the majority of the students coming to the library study their own materials and utilization of the center's materials is largely dependent upon the emphasis the instructor places on its use. That is, to a large degree students do not use library materials unless they are required to do so.

The proper organization of technical services may enhance utilization. Students should have access to all materials through one service, the interfiled card catalog. Although many community colleges are using the Dewey Decimal system of classification, there is a trend for the newly emerging learning resources centers to utilize the Library of Congress Classification System. Overall, there is a variety of means for handling materials of a print and nonprint format in the community colleges throughout the nation.

The emergence of automation in the community college learning resources center may eliminate some problems but create others. Automation will not solve all problems; however, in order to successfully make a wide variety of materials accessible to all users, networks need to be established thus integrating vast resources that would not ordinarily be available.

Chapter VII

LIBRARY TECHNICAL ASSISTANT
NEED, HISTORY OF DEVELOPMENT AND CURRICULUM

The community college curriculum and nature of the learning resources center positions to be staffed brought about the emergence of programs within the community college to meet their needs. More specifically, the effective operation of the learning resources centers, public libraries, university libraries, and school libraries, requires some staff with a technical background who can assume responsibility for those duties that do not require the expertise of a person with a degree in library science or audiovisual education. Library technology and audiovisual technician programs are a natural curriculum offering of the two-year community colleges.

Both library and audiovisual technical programs are being offered at community colleges across the nation; however, there has been little integration of the two areas to form a curriculum for training an all-media technician. Because of its diversity, the audiovisual area selects technicians from electronics, commercial arts, and television in addition to the newly created audiovisual technician programs. The library technician programs have received widespread attention in library circles and the curricula of these programs have been controversial. Since the library technician programs have received this attention and are vitally concerned in the operation of the learning resources center and other libraries, it is the purpose of this chapter to discuss the need for, the history and development of, and the curriculum itself for the training of library technicians. The audiovisual area is not of less importance, but more literature and research connected with the library technician program is availa

For many years professional librarians agreed that there was an acute shortage of professionally trained librarians throughout the country. Unfortunately, there has not been complete agreement as to the need for, or the manner of developing, a middle group of employees between the professional and clerical levels to help solve some of the library manpower problems. However, there are library authorities who advocate the establishment of library technology programs to help narrow the gap between clerical and professional staffs by providing an intermediate level of competently trained library technicians. Such trained library technicians would relieve professional librarians of performing routines and other duties that do not require full professional training. Many professionals, however, believe that a sub-professional or technical class of library employees would constitute a danger to the library profession.

Agnes Stein, an elementary school librarian, concludes: "By the way, what is a librarian? An administrator, a business manager, a technician wired to the AV media, a clerk typing cards and stamping books, a language arts teacher, a public relations man, a storehouse keeper, a bibliophile?"[1]

Are professional librarians spending a portion, sometimes large, of their working day engaged in library work that could be better accomplished by a clerk-typist, or a Library Technical Assistant who has received some formal library training? Much is written and said today about taxpayers' rebellion, cost studies, and accountability in private enterprises and in our public school systems. When will libraries become accountable?

To be recognized by the American Library Association for accreditation, a Library school must meet specific curriculum requirements, staff requirements, and must offer a master's program in Library Science. To meet these requirements, most students will spend a minimum of five years in college. Institutions which offer a major in Library Science within a four-year college program are not accredited library schools because they do not meet the American Library Association standards for the training of professional librarians. In view of the changing economic conditions, it is evident, like it or not, there is, and will be in the future, a definite need for undergraduate library training programs.

Most authors concerned with library education seem to be in relatively close agreement that the basic essentials acquired by a liberal four-year degree followed by a fifth year of librarianship at an American Library Association accredited school are necessary for one to become a professional librarian. There seems to be a general satisfaction among librarians with the equality of training obtained from accredited graduate library schools, but such satisfaction is not the case for the four-year undergraduate library science programs.

Need for Technicians

Competently trained paraprofessionals will make possible maximum use of professionals. Harlow states, "If we could shift 10 percent of what librarians now do to technical and clerical staff, we would have time left equal to fill all of the professional vacancies in the country." To free librarians from clerical work, he recommends the establishment of "a competent corps of assistants at the technical and middle level."[2]

Gebhard states, "Libraries have been forced to hire intelligent persons without library degrees, . . . it would be of great advantage to library service in the United States to give these people more training."[3] In-service training courses, on-the-job training, better utilization of professional staff, and careful selection of subprofessionals from undergraduate library programs have been common means of meeting manpower needs. Unfortunately, most libraries have been forced to use inadequately trained personnel to do work generally considered professional and leave them to do the best job possible.[4]

While it is generally accepted that education for librarianship is long overdue for a basic reorganization, there are many in the library profession who feel that only through the implementation of programs to train library technicians, can the manpower problem at least be partially solved. Traditionally, two main classes of positions in libraries have been recognized, professional and clerical, but this is slowly changing.

"An estimated 76,000 library technicians were employed in 1970; four-fifths were women . . . The employment outlook is excellent for library technicians through the 1970's particularly for graduates of academic programs."[5]

Librarians try to meet the American Library Association and state standards. These efforts, coupled with: (1) the use of federal funds for new kinds of educational programs calling for library services, (2) the increased action by school districts to provide additional elementary school library programs, (3) the move to implement instructional materials centers in more schools, and (4) the increased interest in corporations and other institutions and agencies to have specialized libraries of their own, all add to the need for trained technicians. It is recommended that Community Colleges survey the manpower requirements of their region to determine which colleges might implement new or strengthen existing programs. More effective educational coverage may occur when there is a single strong area program offering not only basic technical education, but additional optional specialized courses.[6]

Nathan Breed of the University of West Virginia offered the following summary relative to the employment of library technical assistants

at the Third Annual Conference of the Council on Library Technology
held in Toledo, Ohio. Through his survey, the following factors
emerged:

(1) Those institutions serving relatively large community areas
     seemed to be most successful in establishing their programs
     and placing their graduates.
(2) The highest salaries offered to the Library Technical
     Assistants were those in positions in Special or Industrial
     Libraries, but that the greatest responsibility placed upon
     the LTA was in the smaller library, especially the school
     and public libraries.
(3) There was considerable disagreement between the LTA and
     the employer when answers were given concerning beginning
     salary levels, and acceptance of the LTA as a bona fide
     library worker by professional staff.[7]

At the same conference, Dr. Newton C. Rochte in his presentation
of the topic "Pioneering a Library Technical Aide Program" stated
that "50% of employees in industry and professions in the 1970's
will be para-professionals!"[8]

Development of Library Technical Programs

Professional librarians for decades have employed nondegree personnel in their institutions. Most of such personnel were designated
library clerks or aides. The larger institutions had an in-service
training program for these persons and some offered formal library
courses. Upon completion of the prescribed courses, the students
were issued a library certificate. The libraries offering library courses
were small in number. The most commonly used method, then and
now, was on-the-job training without any formal library course
work. In the modern library of today, on-the-job training is time

consuming and costly. The library schools of graduate and four-year institutions of higher education have been very adamant against offering a program to train personnel for positions that do not require a professional library degree but do require some training above the requirements for library clerks or aides.

Community colleges saw the need for providing semi-professional training as early as 1949. At that time, Palomar Junior College in California had two courses in library science—books and libraries, and library routines. In 1955, Citrus College in California offered one class in Library Technology. Los Angeles Trade-Technical College offered a course for the training of semi-professional library employees in 1958. The course was successful and the next year a library occupational training program was instituted granting an associate degree. However, between the years of 1949 and 1965 there were less than twenty junior and community colleges in the nation offering courses for the sub-professional.

Considered to be the most comprehensive research literature in the new field of education for library service at that time, the Martinson study indicated in 1965 that: "Most of the programs have existed less than five years and they have all developed pragmatic basis in response to perceived needs in their immediate surroundings. As a result, they do not have a great deal in common and only limited generalizations can be made about the group as a whole.[9] When Martinson completed his survey, there were twenty-six library technician programs operating in the United States.[10]

Since the Martinson study in 1965, there has been a rapid increase in the number of community colleges offering Library Technical Assistants programs. In 1972 there were in thirty-one states of the United States a total of 118 Library Technical Assistants programs offered, and 16 programs were offered in the provinces of Canada.

The first national meeting of those concerned with the education of nonprofessional library assistants was held in Chicago in May 1967. There were forty-seven people at this first meeting. The American Library Association (LED) and some professional librarians present were reluctant to take the Library Technical Assistants Training programs seriously. The professional persons directing the few training programs at that time found it hard to understand why the representatives of ALA rejected the assistant training program at a time when an estimated 100,000 library positions were vacant. Despite lack of enthusiasm in the profession, they did not surrender, and later developed into a national organization with over 100% increase in the number of schools offering Library Technical Assistants Training programs. The national organization the Council on Library Technology, known most commonly as COLT, now has over 200 members with national and regional meetings . (The association has recently been renamed Council on Library Technical-Assistants.)

One of the major concerns of the Council on Library Technology is a standard designation for graduates of the technician programs.

At one time or another several terms have been coined to describe the product of the programs in Library Technology, but no designation has so far seemed to be acceptable to all concerned, but almost at once discussion arose as to its appropriate value.

. . . Within recent months still another term has been used describing the graduate of a program in Library Technology as either LTA or LIBRARY TECHNICAL ASSISTANT. While this latter term seems to be gaining rather wide-spread acceptance, it must be said that it, too, leaves much to be desired as a satisfactory designation.[11]

In the California community colleges, early terminology included library science, library technology, library services, library aide, and library education. The library technician program is now standard throughout the state.

California offers more library technical programs than any other state. A recent California survey indicated thirty-three library technical assistant programs in operation in California community colleges. Also, there were 1,470 full and part-time students enrolled, and 520 of these are expected to receive certificates or associate degrees by June, 1970.[12]

Since junior or community colleges are assuming major responsibility for vocational-technical education, they are the logical source for library training programs at the technician level.

Professional Recognition

There are many difficulties in obtaining recognition for the library technical training program and the graduates of the programs, and in different sections of the United States there continue to be variations in the degree to which library technical assistants are accepted. There seems little doubt that as many assistants as can be trained and graduated can be absorbed by libraries of all kinds. Yet there does not seem to be a consistent pattern of general acceptance.

At the Midwinter meeting in Washington, D.C. in 1965, the American Library Association, Library Education Division Executive Board, approved the following statement relative to the training of library clerks or assistants in junior colleges.

The consensus of Board opinion is that the establishment of courses for the training of library clerks or assistants in junior college should not be encouraged. While there is a need for library technicians and even though some courses are being given, there appears to be no evidence that they have been successful. It was noted that the Personnel Committee of the New York Library Association has recently recommended a proposal for the establishment of undergraduate training programs. There are no standards for such courses.[13]

Dorothy F. Deiniger, *The Deiniger Report*, 1967, presented to
the American Library Association the three following recommendations concerning recognition:

(1)   That two levels of service between clerical and professional
      staff be recognized; namely, the library clerk and the library
      technical assistant. Classification standards for these levels
      and typical duties have been proposed for consideration.

(2)   That the Library Education Division and Library Admini-
      stration Division recognize the value of the vocational train-
      ing for library clerks and library technical assistants and
      appoint a committee to develop curricula and standards
      for training which would strengthen existing and planned
      programs and divert efforts into Association proved
      channels which will contribute to library manpower ob-
      jectives. . . .

(3)   That a committee be established to make a concerted effort
      to clarify and correct definitions and scope of typical
      library occupations in the U.S. Department of Labor pub-
      lication, "Directory of Occupational Titles" in occupation-
      al literature, in vocational guidance materials, and in con-
      nection with advertised goals of library training offered
      in vocational schools and junior colleges, whether they
      are private, state or municipal institutions.[14]

At the Second Annual Conference of the Council on Library
Technology held in Toledo, Ohio, May, 1968, Dr. Lester Asheim,
Library Education Division, American Library Association, com-
mented on the training of library assistants.

There is no official A.L.A. position at present concerning
training library assistants at the junior college level. He went on
to point out that while he conceded that the theory behind the

use of library aides is sound, he felt that many of the objections
to the training of library technicians which had been expressed
in 1965 were still valid. He pointed out that he did not question
the need for a supporting staff for libraries, but that the question
is at what level they are needed, and what kind of preparation
should they have.[15]

The California State Department of Education made the following comments in their publication *Multi-Media and the Changing
School Library* as early as 1959.

The presently developing program of the State Department of
Education to establish a uniform library technician training program in California is strongly endorsed as a means of providing
needed library technical assistants for semi- or para-professional
and clerical staffing in school libraries. This program includes
terminal courses to enable students to serve at various job levels
in the school library, to provide technical services for effective
and efficient library operation, and to free professional school
librarians for other more important work.[16]

Yet in 1967 and later, library literature included articles pointing
out the danger of professional librarians being replaced by technician program graduates capable of accomplishing tasks which
normally occupy much of a librarian's time. In one reputable
library magazine, an article was featured which referred to institutions offering library technical programs as "peddlers of educational snake oil."[17]

It is true that many professional librarians fear the Library Technical Assistants may take their positions. At many meetings where
the role of the Library Technical Assistants is discussed it is evident that this fear exists mostly by employed personnel who are
not in the American Library Association terminology considered

professional librarians. It is important that better communications be established stating precisely the work the Library Technical Assistants have been trained to administer. This would eliminate a lot of the fears.

Professional librarians should not be concerned about technicians filling positions in libraries which should be held by graduate librarians. If professional librarianship is necessary in a position then an individual lacking the professional background and training will be unable to fill the position. If the professional is in a job which can be performed by graduates of a two-year program, then he should not be doing the job.

> To view Community College library technical assistant preparation as a basic preparation for a career ladder, however, is still a debatable question among librarians and other educators . . . The Council requests the Director and Council staff, in cooperation with representatives from the University, the State Colleges, and the Junior Colleges to formulate a plan for review of new programs which will provide for both the orderly growth of higher education and involve the Council as early as possible. . . .[18]

At the Council of Library Technology held at Toledo, Ohio, Mrs. Rhua Heckart responded to comments from speakers and panel members at the conference. She strongly held that library aides, when properly trained, can only upgrade the entire library profession. She pointed out that the programs [were] less than three years old, but she said that some of the older programs are able to provide such information. It was Mrs. Heckart's position that not only do we need to define the role of the library technician, but that the definition of the library professional needs redefining as well.[19]

Although recognition for library technical courses for the training and employment of library supportive personnel has not been widely accepted by professional librarians, and within library associations, considerable progress has been made in many areas in the last five years. In January 1969, the Library Education Division of the American Library Association developed a document on training programs for supportive library staff to serve as a guide for persons planning programs. The programs were conceived as introductory preparation of personnel to fill beginning positions in the range of library technical assistant positions in a variety of situations.[20]

Articulation between junior and community colleges offering library technical assistants programs and universities offering the professional library degree is making considerable progress in the State of California as well as other states.

The increased employment of the library technical assistant graduate by industrial libraries, public libraries, college and university libraries, and school libraries indicates that such training is fulfilling a need.

Certification, Curriculum and Job Descriptions

Although considerable progress has been made in recognition, training, and employment of library technical programs and library technical assistants, there remains considerable planning and implementation of guidelines and standards for institutions offering the curriculum.

The library technology programs across the nation have been organized by each institution offering the program without coordination with other institutions. The number of semester hours offered in library technical programs by institutions in the United States range from three to thirty-six. There is no standardization of titles or of course content. Recommendations have been made that, as a starting point, institutions within a state offering library technical programs adopt a statewide policy for a uniform sequence of courses. Such a policy would benefit students who transfer from

one college to another. A standardization of course titles and
curricula would help the professional librarians who employ the
technicians. Evaluation of graduates from such a program would
be much easier if an employer could rely on the consistency of
the applicant's training. Standardization in this area would contribute to consistency.

Emphasis for the need of uniformity in library technical programs comes from the California School Library Workshop for
Leadership Personnel. The committee that studied pre-service and
in-service training programs stated that "The presently developing
program of the State Department of Education to establish a uniform library technician training program in California junior
colleges is strongly endorsed as a means of providing needed
library technical assistants for (semi) paraprofessional and clerical
staffing in school libraries."[21]

A superficial survey of seventy-five institutions was made by the
editor of Council on Library Technology in 1968 and the following
information was received relative to the types of courses offered:

Course Title	Number Offered
Introduction to Librarianship	53
Reference Books and Materials	53
Acquisitions, Book Selections and Technical Processes	44
Practice Work	28
Cataloging and Classification	25
Audio-Visual: Acquisition and Preparation	20
Circulation	12
Children's Literature	12
Data Processing	7
Library Problems	5

Story Telling   3

Nine other miscellaneous course
   titles   2 or fewer[22]

The library technology program at Illinois Central College, East Peoria, Illinois offers an associate in applied science degree for students interested in working in libraries as library technical assistants. The curriculum is designed to provide the student with a general educational background as well as specialized training for library work under the supervision of a professional librarian. The curriculum for the degree includes four full semesters of classroom work. To qualify for admission the student must be a high school graduate and in good physical health. Students who do not wish to take the degree program may take only the library and audiovisual courses. (See Appendix C)

It should be made clear that the training discussed does not apply to the library clerk classifications which do not require formal academic training in library subjects. Clerk's assignments are based upon general clerical and secretarial proficiencies. Familiarity with basic library terminology and routine necessary to adapt clerical skills to the library's need is best learned on the job.

The library technical assistant should be trained to assume certain kinds of specific "technical" skills. Educational institutions of today encompass much more than just the printed media. Closed circuit television, 16 mm films, information retrieval systems, audio and video tapes, 2 x 2 slides, transparencies, programmed instruction, and microfilm are examples of mass media that have been added to the printed materials. Consequently, library technical assistant training programs should include courses in audiovisual education.

Library technical assistants are not meant simply to perform advanced clerical work. While clerical skills might well be a part of a technical assistant's equipment, the emphasis in his assignment should be on the special technical skill. For example, someone who is skilled in handling audiovisual equipment, introductory processing, or in making posters and other displays might well be employed in the technical assistant category for these skills, related to librarianship only to the extent that they are employed in a library.

Thornton Community College, Harvey, Illinois does not offer a program for library technical assistants but offers an associate degree for the educational media technician and a certificate program for the educational media technician, composed of largely audiovisual courses. (See Appendix C)

The Office of the Chancellor, California Community Colleges, offers the following six steps in developing a library technical assistant curriculum:

(1)   Conduct a study of manpower requirements on a Community College area of planning basis. It may not be practical for every college to offer a program. It is recommended that colleges consider developing strong specialized programs where students can be referred through interdistrict agreements.

(2)   Establish an advisory committee for the program. The committee should help plan for the initial curriculum and evaluate programs. In addition to local professional library representatives from each of the various types of libraries, the committee should include representation from local and county personnel offices, a four-year academic institution, and a library association.

(3)   Adopt a curriculum to meet the needs of the community by setting definite achievement levels that are geared to the competencies required for job entry into the field.

(4)   Continually evaluate the program to insure that it meets

state and national standards and its stated goals.

(5) Develop a structured work experience education program that has a direct relationship to the classroom program.

(6) Communicate freely with the appropriate college administrators and the state and national library associations.[23]

The Office of the Chancellor also states:

There are two categories which must be served with regard to
the training of library technicians and their involvement with
audiovisual materials and equipment.
These two categories are:

(1) The training of the library technician to meet the occasional
audio-visual needs which may arise in the relatively "traditional" library where non-book or audio-visual materials
are not emphasized . . .

(2) The training of the library technician to meet the demands
of a "total media" library program where an expertise in
handling audio-visual services is a basic requirement thus
calling for special training in audio-visual methods and
processes.[24]

With 118 institutions in the United States offering library technical assistant courses, with the wide variation in number of semester
hours required at each institution, and with little standardization
of courses, it seems evident that there is a definite need for job
classifications and for some type of local, regional and national
recognition on certification.

Potentially, there is no doubt that the library technical assistant
will be in demand and that the role of the LTA will be better defined and skills refined. There is a unique place, distinctly different
from the competent school librarian or public librarian or academic

librarian for LTAs. It is a role which will become clearer as more
technical assistants are trained and employed.

Assignments for the library technical assistant were stated in
1968 by the Interdivisional Ad Hoc Committee of the Library
Education Division and the Library Administrative Division as
follows:

> *Scope of Assignments.* Typical duties include supervision of
> library clerk or clerical staff in performance of duties in the
> area of assignment. He may perform specialized library clerical
> duties, such as descriptive cataloging, interlibrary loan or acqui-
> sitions work, help readers in using catalog, locate simple biblio-
> graphic information, answer directional questions, be in charge
> of department, such as circulation or reserve collection. . . .
> *Personal Contacts.* Many positions require supervision of other
> employees and a work relationship with the library's clientele
> and business associates. . . .
> *Level of Responsibility.* He deals with a wide variety of situ-
> ations including frequent public and personal contacts and relies
> to a large extent on staff manuals or established policies, fre-
> quently requesting advice of his supervisor. . . .[25]

The best and clearest statement is the report (1969) entitled
"Criteria for Programs to Prepare Library Technical Assistants."[26]
This report is important because it gives distinguishing character-
istics for the several categories of library staff.

> The criteria suggested in the federal civil service Position Classi-
> fication Standards offer a very good basis for distinguishing be-
> tween the general clerical and the library aide positions. In the
> federal standards it is recognized that a non-academic worker
> must use clerical skills such as typing and filing whether he be
> assigned to the general clerical or to the library clerical classi-

fication. The distinguishing element is the characteristic which
is of paramount importance in performing the job.[27]

The federal civil service pattern thus has seven, or possibly
more, non-academic library employee levels. Library Aides occupy the levels GS-4 to GS-7. Under certain circumstances a
Library Technician can be assigned an even higher level.

No job is exactly the same in all situations. The librarian performs
and will perform in the future some jobs which are not purely
professional. A library clerk will perform some jobs which may
be technical. Technicians will perform some jobs which are
clerical and some that may be professional.

Job descriptions, certification and curriculum for library technical assistant training programs have made considerable progress
in the past four years. However, continuous work by institutions
offering the program must continue to attempt standardization
of the job classifications, to establish salary ranges, and to achieve
certification.

Summary

Many libraries and learning resources centers have been forced
to seek solutions other than master's degreed personnel for staffing.
One solution has been the preparation of the library and audiovisual technical assistant. Professional librarians, on the other hand,
are receiving severe criticism from all sides for spending a large
amount of their time doing routine work of a clerical or subprofessional nature.

Recent studies indicate a large and increasing need for library
personnel to work in positions between the level of the professional
librarian and the library clerk. They should have academic library
training on a level below that of the professional librarians. Community colleges are in agreement with these studies and during the

past seven years, 118 have been offering library technical courses for training library technical assistants.

In the early development of the junior and community college training of library technical assistants, the American Library Association, many professional librarians, and the professional library training institutions looked with skepticism upon these sub-professional training programs. This skepticism was justified in most cases because the programs offered differed widely from institution to institution and state to state.

With the feeling that there is a need for the library technical assistant and the continued offering of courses by the two-year institutions of higher education, the American Library Association, Council on Library Technology, and other library professional groups have been planning and working to establish standard training courses, job descriptions, job classifications, and certification for the library technical assistant's training and employment. The continued improvement of the library technical assistant status in the library profession will provide better service for patrons of learning resources centers as well as a more clearly defined role for the trained professional librarian.

Chapter VIII

A BUILDING PROGRAM FOR NEW FACILITIES

One of the major items in the building program of a new campus is the learning resources center. The center should not only house the library but the audiovisual facilities, and could include remedial or self-instructional laboratories. In this chapter the development and design of a functional building program for a community college learning resources center serving approximately 5,000 full-time-equivalent students is discussed. This hypothetical center will be able to house at least 60,000 volumes and contains seating for approximately 25 per cent of the student body. The emphasis of this discussion is on general concepts of planning, the philosophy, spatial relationships, and the functions of space allocations.

General Concepts

Planning a new facility or renovating an old one is too large an undertaking for a single person. Planning on most campuses should and will include administrators, consultants, faculty, trustees, and students. Although each group may not be specifically involved in the intricate planning from the beginning, its expertise constitutes a major contribution. The responsibility of the director of the learning resources center is to collect data from all contributors and coordinate all efforts into the building plan. Martin Van Buren noted in 1960 that the librarian has a vital role in three critical stages of planning and the development of the facility: the written program, the architectural floor plan, and the final list of furnishings and equipment.[1] Before further discussing the learning resources center director's role and the institution's philosophy, some general considerations concerning planning should be analyzed.

In *A Guide for Planning Community Junior College Facilities* (1969), the following suggestions are given: "Each part of the instructional center must be carefully planned to secure the greatest possible economy and efficiency. The reading rooms, carrels, listening and viewing rooms, book stacks, offices, conference rooms, work rooms, and equipment storage rooms must all be planned to meet both immediate and future needs. No other part of the campus is likely to undergo greater change than the instructional center."[2]

According to Keyes Metcalf, "the greatest mistakes are the result of decisions made by those who do not understand the implications of those decisions—functionally, financially, and aesthetically."[3] Further commenting upon the requirements of a library, Metcalf had made, in 1965, the following generalizations which continue to be as valid as when stated.

(1) Since physical changes of many kinds can be expected to take place as the years go by, the utmost flexibility is required.

(2) Since increase in space demands for collections and reader accommodations is almost inevitable, a building, if it is to continue to be useful must be so placed and planned that it can be readily enlarged.

(3) Since accommodations will rise in quality, at least as far as those for the comfort of the occupant and preservation of the collections are concerned, over-economizing is unwise.[4]

The library is constantly changing. One of the most far-reaching changes of the last two decades is the growing importance of the unified materials concept. Another change affecting building plans is the importance of the individual and his needs. For instance, Alvin Toffler, in an introduction to *Bricks and Mortar Boards,* predicts that the age of the clean-lined contemporary library with an emphasis in efficiency and economy is over. "Campus planners, architects, and librarians are modifying its principles, softening the lines of the revolutionary model, adding grace to its form, and shaping the library to accommodate man in all his individual variety. The result is a more human library than any we have ever known."[5]

At the same time, technological advances provide an ever increasing quantity of printed materials, as well as continuing changes in the format of learning materials. The electronic age has put many previously unavailable items at our fingertips, and a basic question is, how do these changes affect facilities planning? "The avalanche of technological discoveries, the accelerating pace of change may, as has been suggested, transform the library, eliminate the book, and still-unthought-of methods for collecting, storing, recovering, and communicating information. But for the foreseeable future, the campus library with all its primitive faults, will remain a vital part of our intellectual landscape."[6]

Philosophy

As so often stated, the philosophy of each institution should reflect the needs of those it serves. No one philosophical statement can reflect all schools, for priorities vary as institutions vary. Consequently, before planning can become specific, it is important to determine the relationship of the learning resources center to the total instructional effort. The following questions should be answered: "Should it be centralized or decentralized? Should the entire college be a library or should there be no center at all? Should the center be separate and identifiable or integrated into the total structure? Is the center the means of instruction or is it an aid to instruction? What about security? The hardware, another big question; is it the servant or the master? What tasks can it best do, and how is it interphased to other systems in the school, community, or region?"[7]

How important is the individual? If the direction of the institution is to serve the individual, then the planning for the educational facility should provide for:

Encouragement of individual initiative, responsibility and motivation, so that learning becomes person-centered rather than people-centered.

Development of individual interests and special abilities to allow the individual to establish his appropriate and useful role in society.

Accommodation of differing individual capacities for learning as well as social and economic backgrounds within the total framework of formal education.

Development of a sense of personal identification and participation in the learning process, as well as basic learning skills which may be applied in personal learning and self education.[8]

Will the center have an active commitment to instruction? A summary follows of the library as a teaching instrument on the college campus:

Students have direct access to many carriers of knowledge so that they can develop judgment in selecting the most relevant, and so that they can learn to distinguish between the good and the bad.

Students are individuals. As such they have individual needs in working with the carriers. The library arranges its facilities, both human and physical, to give each student an opportunity to work alone.

Because the physical environment has much to do with the behavior of the student, the library strives to be comfortable, friendly, and inviting.

Every means is tried for motivating students to read. The strongest motive has been found to come from the interaction of teacher and student in the classroom.[9]

The role of the traditional library is changing. It seems imperative to focus upon the individual who can discriminate between successful and unsuccessful modes of communication in a changing environment. The center should be developed within the philosophy of the institution; its major source of support will be drawn from that philosophy.

Foothill College District in California, a community college district, has developed at least two campuses with libraries at each. Five areas of their philosophy as established in early planning phases follow:

Purpose—The library is the instructional materials center of the college, providing books, periodicals and other printed materials, audio and visual material to implement the curriculum, to provide recreational and cultural materials, and to aid instructors in teaching.

Facilities—Its facilities and physical features must provide for differences in tastes, abilities, and needs, offering a wide range of materials and providing spaces for quiet individual research, group study, listening, viewing and recreational reading.

Arrangement—For effective, economical operation it is desirable to separate noisy functions from quiet areas and to group together services requiring specialized training to administer.

Atmosphere—The building must look like a library and have an attractive, informal, orderly appearance in order to develop in its patrons an appreciation and enjoyment of its materials and services in order to fulfill the objectives of the college, since its use is not specifically required or scheduled.

Development—The building must allow for expansion and change with few structural modifications.[10]

An additional consideration in the development of a philosophy is the general pattern of user service to be provided in the learning resources center. Based upon an understanding of functions, the determination of spatial relationships constitutes the next step in planning.

Spatial Relationships and General Requirements

The purpose and nature of this portion of the building program is to illustrate verbally and visually the relationships and operation of the various functions of the learning resources center. For instance, how does the card catalog relate to the circulation desk and what special considerations should be given to each area? Metcalf states that ". . . these relationships, which have a close connection with the organization and service pattern of a library, must be clearly stated in the program, because the architect, even if he is acquainte with library procedures, would otherwise have no way of knowing any special relationships desired by the librarian and his staff."[11]

Ralph Ellsworth has noted that there are five basic relationships which are common to college libraries:

(1)   There should be one central exit control point at which all who leave the building can be checked to make certain the library materials they are taking out have been properly checked out.

(2)   As soon as the reader has passed the vestibule, he goes into a lobby, a place the architect uses for various purposes: a center for displays, to quiet down readers as they come into the building, to lead the reader to the key library books and operations, to house new book exhibits, and even as a place for receptions.

(3)   Immediately beyond the lobby we should see the tools and services that serve as keys—catalog, reference services, bibliographies—to the library.

(4) Traffic patterns should be planned so that as one enters
     a building he can use the cloak room, locker check room,
     and toilets before he passes the control exit point.
(5) Provisions for books and readers will be dependent on two
     factors: (a) the type of building–fixed function vs. modu-
     lar; and, (b) the type of organization to be used.[12]

Metcalf, in turn, asks more general questions concerning these
relationships as they pertain to the community college:

(1) What public services should be close to the entrance lobby?
(2) Should the quarters for the processing department be on
     the level with the services in 1 above?
(3) What should be the relationships, as far as space assign-
     ments are concerned, between the shipping and receiving
     rooms and the acquisition department?
(4) Should the administrative officers be on the same level
     with central services?
(5) How important is it to place a large percentage of seating
     accommodations in the entrance level . . .?[13]

Library
   A spatial relationship diagram of the library functions of the
learning resources center includes the following areas: lobby, offices,
circulation, periodical area, technical services, card catalog, reference
area, reading and study area, stacks, faculty reading area, typing
facility, microfilm reading area, group study facilities, and receiving
and storage. A visual diagram of these relationships is presented in
Table 2. This diagram will change from institution to institution
as reflected in their differing philosophies.
   The lobby should be the central point of entry for both students
and faculty. It should be the branching point upon entering the
facility as persons will be channeled to the library, the audiovisual
center, the basic skills laboratory, and the television facilities.

Table 2

SPATIAL RELATIONSHIPS—LIBRARY

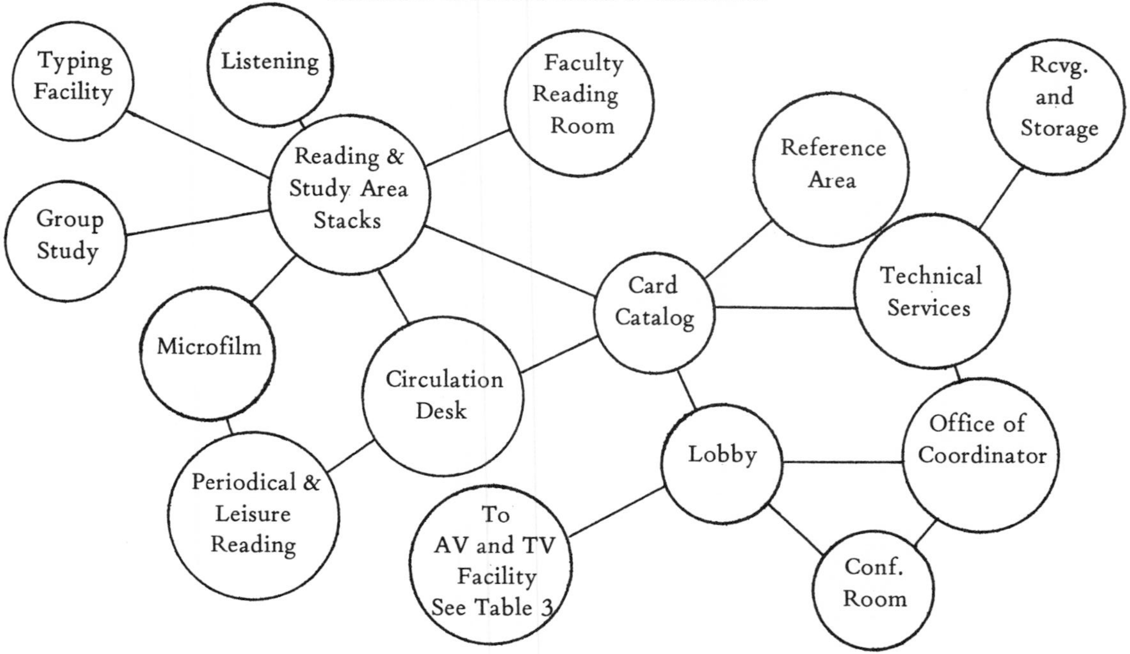

The lobby is an ideal facility for leisure seating and exhibit and display areas.

Adjacent or in close proximity to the lobby should be the circulation desk. Its location should provide a check point for persons leaving the facility; however, it should not seriously hamper traffic flow patterns. Provision should be made for conduit allowing for future utilization of electronic data processing equipment. The circulation desk should be of modular flexible construction to enable the size to be enlarged or to allow the shifting of the internal components as persons establish work habits. The library patrons also may develop utilization patterns which could result in needed modification. In the community college, it is recommended that the circulation desk be extremely flexible.

The card catalog has a close relationship with and should be situated near the following: circulation desk, technical services, and the reference area. It should be easily accessible.

The reading and study area should be integrated with the main stack area. The user should be able to proceed to these areas without obstructions from the circulation desk or card catalog. Certain community college librarians prefer that the circulation desk have an unobstructed view of these study areas; however, it is not in the authors' opinion a necessity. Seating should be provided in carrels and tables with small sections of leisure seating interdispersed. There is a tendency to provide individual rather than group seating whenever possible. Book storage in many community colleges is provided in mezzanine areas, thus allowing the student to go to one specific area for all book materials.

The reference area provides for student research. It should be efficiently arranged, not as a separate facility but integrated within the reading and study areas. The reference librarian should be easily accessible for the inquiring student, not in a separate walled area.

The periodical reading area, containing current subscriptions, should be integrated with the student reading area, not be set aside as a specific room. Back issues for the current year may be stored in this area also. However, bound periodicals or microfilm may, in many cases, be stored separately in the regular book stacks, a separate room, or in a microfilm viewing area respectively.

The microfilm viewing area, containing microfilm and microfiche of periodicals and other research materials, should be located in close proximity to the periodical reading and storage area. Although it does not necessarily warrant a separate room, less illumination is needed in this area and it may be the preference of the librarian to house this service in a special facility.

Typing facilities should be available to students for general purposes, housed in a room that is sound resistant and wired for electric typewriters. The room should be adjacent to the reading areas. An unobstructed view from the circulation area may be desired.

Group study areas consisting of small conference rooms should be generously provided adjacent to reading areas. These rooms allow students and faculty to hold informal discussions or small seminars without leaving the facility. Group study areas should be arranged so that visual supervision from the circulation desk is possible.

A room for the institution's instructional staff should be provided. Such a faculty room should be designed for both leisure and scholarly reading, and shall contain current professional periodicals and books. In some institutions, this facility will be supplemented with additional faculty offices housed within the learning resources center. An area for the supportive staff of the center is also desirable for staff use during work breaks, meal breaks and other activities

The technical services area serves as the central receiving and processing area for materials in print and non-print formats. Because of the number of staff working in this area, it should be located near the coordinator of the library's office. The technical services area also must have direct access to the card catalog. Furthermore, because of staffing difficulties it perhaps should be located near the circulation desk; in many community colleges, the limited staff requires that at peak periods technical staff perform other duties as the need arises.

Audiovisual

The consideration of spatial relationships of the audiovisual facility of the learning resources center is also important; some community colleges may separate audiovisual facilities within the learning resources center complex, others may integrate all media in one facility. In the following discussion, no areas are planned for large group instruction although some colleges may include a large group instruction facility in the center. The planning of production and support facilities and classrooms for independent study within the facility must take into account the fact that many independent study activities do not take place in the formal classroom. Some factors to be considered are:

(1)   No student will spend all his time in independent study and not all students can handle independence.

(2)   Independent study needs to be complemented by group activities, particularly seminar and project situations which allow a small group to share experiences.

(3)   Programs utilizing a high degree of independent study place special demands on the teacher, support staff, administration, resources and facilities.[14]

In designing facilities for the production of and access to nonprint material, the following factors should be considered:

(1)   Production and support functions and in turn their facilities vary in complexity and size with their location and level within the educational system.

(2)   Production support centers may be composed of a variety

of components, each of which is related according to the echelon of production and the types of service to be offered.

(3) The instructional support center can perform several major services in addition to producing films, slides, tapes, and other instructional materials.

(4) Instructional support facilities may be an integral part of an educational plant, or may be a separate, free-standing building or unit.

(5) One of the changes anticipated above involves the planning of TV studios.

(6) Obviously there is no single instructional support facility which solves all needs at all levels.[15]

A spatial relationship diagram of a separate audiovisual facility within the center includes areas for lobby, reception and scheduling, storage and repair, graphics and production, television, basic skills laboratory, preview rooms, recording studies and a darkroom. A visual arrangement of these facilities is represented by Table 3.

The lobby should be jointly utilized and incorporated with the main lobby of the learning resources center. Leading directly from the lobby should be a reception and scheduling area. Thus when a student or faculty member enters the audiovisual complex, he can be directed to the appropriate area. If he is interested in scheduling a film or equipment for later classroom use, he can accomplish his task here. It is through this area one gains access to the audiovisual complex.

The graphics and production facility provides equipment for production and reproduction of visual and audio materials for the total campus community. A darkroom should be an integral part of this area as well as preview rooms and an audio recording studio. Ideally, this facility should be in close proximity to the area devoted to television.

Table 3

SPATIAL RELATIONSHIPS—AUDIOVISUAL

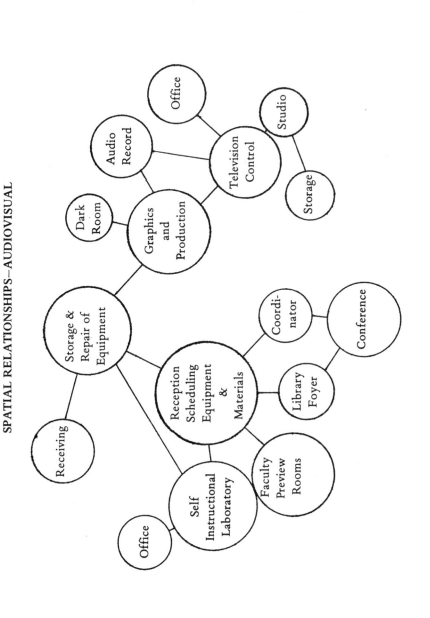

The storage and repair areas are chiefly devoted to maintaining and repairing equipment. They also serve as a central receiving area for audiovisual supplies and equipment.

A listening and audio retrieval facility may be planned for the distribution of tape or disc program materials to stations within the learning resources center and to specified locations on campus. The area should also include a control room for location of the hardware needed for distribution of programs. (Colleges may want to delete this area because of expense.)

The television control and studio should be able to produce and distribute video programs throughout the campus. This facility should be closely situated with audio retrieval control and the graphics area. A storage area for television props should be located adjacent to the studio.

The self instructional laboratory has as its primary goal the improve ment of study skills needed for successful completion of the degree programs. The area should house audiovisual hardware for self instruction along with programmed texts. Preferably access to this facility should be through the lobby since there will be heavy studen use.

In close proximity to the scheduling and reception area should be preview facilities for students and faculty to allow previewing without increasing traffic through other audiovisual areas.

In the preceding discussion concerning the spatial relationships and major functions of audiovisual activities within the learning resources center, it should be noted that the language laboratory and reading laboratory were excluded. If the philosophy and needs of a particular college so dictate, these activities can also be incorporated within the center.

It should be noted that the relationships illustrated in Tables 2 and 3 are not the *only* emerging patterns of development, and each community college should develop their own patterns as reflected by the needs of the particular institution and community.

Recommended Space Requirements

Because of changing technologies and the individual philosophies of specific institutions, space requirements for the learning resources center of colleges will vary considerably. Ralph Ellsworth, commenting upon the uncertainty of change within library buildings, points out that "All we really know is that we should provide a good deal of uncommitted floor space that can accommodate rooms of varying size, each well-lighted, properly ventilated, with access to wiring ducts from which electrically powered machines can draw their power, with good soundproofing qualities. . . . Our buildings should be capable of major expansion or of conversion to other uses."[16] Can a helpful determination be made to specify the space required for each facility?

Library

The reading and stack storage areas have as their major purposes the storage of printed materials and the accommodations for the reading public. A unified effort of library planning in concise form has been put together in *Manual Four "Academic Support Facility"* by the Western Interstate Commission for Higher Education.[17] A generally acceptable standard indicates that approximately 25 per cent of the student body (full-time-equivalent) should have seating accommodations and that twenty-five square feet is an acceptable standard per reader. With these guidelines in mind, it requires at least 31,250 square feet to accommodate readers for an institution of 5,000 full-time-equivalent students 25% of 5,000 FTE (1,250 X 25 sq. ft. = 31,250). In a 1966 summary of proposed standards in California, the recommendations were slightly lower in that only 15-20 per cent of the student population was to be seated.[18] The ratio of carrels, leisure seating, and tables should be determined by the institution. However, Keyes Metcalf states ". . . that today if it were done, I'd go to 75 or 80 per cent individualized seating—and this for undergraduates."[19]

An average number of volumes, for 5,000 full-time-equivalent students, may be 60,000. The California standards indicate that .10 assignable square feet of space are required per volume,[20] but Metcalf proposes an alternate plan, determining space by the number of volumes per range of stacks.[21] According to California standards space required for book storage will be approximately 6,000 square feet. In addition, the California standards recommend that another 25 per cent of the space allocated for book storage be allowed for special collections.[22] Therefore, an additional 1,500 square feet should be provided bringing the total to 7,500 square feet for shelving of all book materials.

In library planning space must be allowed also for staff requirements. A generally acceptable allocation is approximately 125 square feet per person. The California State College Standards require at least 100 square feet for each full-time library staff position and specifies a range from 80 to 160 square feet depending on position function.[23] Another formula for computing space would provide a basic complement of 400 assignable square feet plus 140 assignable square feet per full-time-equivalent staff.[24] Using this formula, 1,800 square feet would be required for ten positions. In the community college, additional space should be allocated for technical services. Although in most cases, this is included with the staff requirements, an additional 1,000 square feet should be provided plus additional space for staff at the above recommended level.

Additional space requirements should include a typing room, microfilm reading and storage, and a staff reading room and lounge. Metcalf recommends at least fifteen gross square feet for each employee in a staff room, so at least 300 square feet should be provided considering growth.

The library would not be complete without conference rooms for students and faculty to interact. Each conference room should contain approximately 150 square feet, and at least six such rooms are needed.

Audiovisual

As yet there have been few standards established with respect to the space required for housing the audiovisual facility. Perhaps the best unified effort has been made through WICHE by condensing the findings of the Office of the Vice Chancellor, State University of New York.

Facility Function or Category	Two Year Colleges		
	1 to 3,000 FTE	3,001 to 5,000 FTE	5,001 to 7,000 FTE
Core Service			
Graphics	800	800	800
Photography	600	800	1,020
Equipment and Materials Circulation	1,000	1,400	1,640
Equipment Maintenance	400	400	400
Studios	1,200	1,500	1,500
T.V. Audio Distribution	1,200	1,200	1,200
Audio Services and Radio	480	600	800
Shops and Storage	1,400	1,600	1,800
Administration	480	600	840
Instructional Development	540	860	1,000
Total Assignable Square Feet	8,100	9,760	11,000[26]

Two areas which need further consideration are the listening and audio-video retrieval area, and the self instructional laboratory. Both these facilities will involve a multitude of activities and should include approximately 1,200 square feet each.

Summary of Spatial Requirements

As previously noted, the guidelines used in this chapter are only points for preliminary planning in a learning resources center. The real space allocations will be determined by the philosophy of the institution and the budget on which it has to operate. An example of space requirements is found in Table 4.

Other Considerations in Planning

Carpet

Within many facilities the question of whether to carpet or not will arise. Since the initial cost of carpet is somewhat higher than other floor coverings and it has been considered a luxury in the past, its advantages need careful study. The library technology project has listed the following advantages:

(1)   Acoustical properties—carpet is outstanding in this respect.
(2)   Maintenance—the cost of maintaining a given area of carpeting is considerably less than that of maintaining a comparable area of resilient tile.
(3)   Decor—carpeting adds a feeling of luxury, warmth, and friendliness.
(4)   Psychological—carpeting creates an atmosphere conducive to study.[27]

The Educational Facilities laboratory has projected that within a six to eight-year period, the saving in maintenance is expected to offset the difference in initial cost.[28]

Table 4

SPACE NEEDS FOR LRC WITH 5,000 FTE STUDENTS

A. Library (excluding lobby)
   1) Student stations (1,250 (25% of 5,000 FTE) X
      25 sq. ft. = 31,250)   31,250
   2) Area needed for printed materials storage:
      Book storage   6,000
      Special collection   1,500
   3) Staff requirements (10 positions)   1,800
   4) Processing and technical services (5 staff)   1,700
   5) Typing   350
   6) Microfilm reading and storage   350
   7) Staff reading room and lounge   300
   8) Group study rooms (6 at 150 square feet)   900
                                                              44,150

B. Audiovisual and Television   11,000

C. Listening and Audio-Video retrieval   1,200

D. Self Instructional Laboratory   1,200

GRAND TOTAL   57,550

The American Carpet Institute has summarized the effects of
carpet in the following statement:

We have shown some of the ways carpeting blends with education's drive for excellence and its need for economy . . . the
superior acoustical qualities of the carpeted classroom, for example, and the ease and economy with which a carpeted classroom can be maintained. These are tangible qualities whose value
to education is readily measured and demonstrated. Carpeting
also possesses an intangible quality of significant value: this is
its aesthetic quality . . . its warmth, its color, its elegant texture.
To be sure, we cannot measure this quality. We can only note

that it inevitably adds dignity to any room, whether the living room at home or the classroom at school. Is there a room more worthy of that dignity than one whose purpose is to teach a child?[29]

Lighting
One does not have to closely examine the interior of a well-planned learning resources center to note the adequacy of its lighting. According to Blackwell, ". . . bad lighting, which reduces the effectiveness of information collection, can lead to localized or general discomfort."[30]

"The decision of what lighting to use in a library should be based not upon whether the source is fluorescent, incandescent, polarized, or any other type of arbitrarily high level lighting, but rather upon the comfort that can be obtained without confusing brightness, contrasts or glare."[31]

Metcalf summarizes his discussion of lighting with the following:

(1)   . . . high-intensity light of poor quality is less desirable than low-intensity light of good quality.
(2)   Every effort within reason should be made to improve the quality of visual atmosphere.
(3)   An intensity of 50 foot-candles on the reading surface should be satisfactory for all but the most exacting reading tasks in a library.
(4)   Twenty-five to 30 foot-candles should be sufficient in most library reading areas so long as 50 are readily available in some areas and 75 in a very few places . . .[32]

Seating
With the rise in importance of the individual in library planning, the question of individual seating is of primary importance. This individual importance is reflected in many instances in the replace-

ment of the table by the carrel. Ralph Ellsworth said, "It has been proven over and over again in college libraries that students don't like to read in large open reading rooms. They like the privacy and the intimacy of small groups. They do not want to sit at flat tables in the middle of a large reading room."[33]

However, Sommer stated that privacy should not be the sole or major goal of library design. "Though it is a major factor to be taken into account in planning individual study areas, there are other parts of the library where informal and spontaneous inter-action can be encouraged."[34]

Ellsworth further suggested that planners should use the follow-ing guidelines for allocating seating:

70% in the form of carrels
10% in the form of regular library tables
10% in the form of group study rooms
 5% in the form of seminars
 5% in the form of lounge type chairs[35]

Thus despite continuing divergence of recommendations, greater emphasis is being placed upon seating for the individual in carrels.

Automation

Within the next decade, vast changes will occur in information distribution within most community college campuses. Automated circulation, bibliographical control, mechanization of technical services, "wet" carrels, audio retrieval, and television distribution are examples of progress which is currently being made. At this point, it would be unwise to specify detailed items for particular areas because technologies are in constant change. In order to adapt to the changing environment, the new facility and campus should provide a network of raceways for conduit connecting all outlaying buildings to allow for distribution of programs or the establishment of terminals.

In *Libraries of the Future*, Licklider wrote "It is difficult, of course, to think about man's interaction with recorded knowledge at so distant a time. Very great and pertinent advances doubtless can be made during the remainder of this century, both in information technology and in the ways man uses it."[36]

Robert Blackburn reporting on automation and building plans indicated that the planners will react in a variety of ways to what the effects will be on the building program. "To be absolutely safe, of course, in the face of present uncertainties, a library should tell its architect to go away and come back in twenty years, when more is known."[37]

As witnessed by these two quotations, changes will continue to transform learning resources center activities and area needs. For this reason, the campus community needs to share resources in order to unify the automated system and not operate competing services.

Summary

Some basic considerations in planning a new learning resources center have been discussed above. Planning is a time consuming effort and cannot be accomplished overnight. "A lead time of not less than three years beyond the date of occupancy appears to be a reasonable minimum for the typical junior college."[38]

The needs in terms of meeting the objectives of the institution are paramount in planning a building program. Philosophy, spatial relationships, and the space needed for operations are vital elements in the program.

"The building program is to the architect as the lesson plan is to the classroom teacher; without it the result can be ineffective and wasteful. All that goes into any building is the best informed knowledge brought to bear by the group concerned with it."[39]

As presented in this chapter, there are no set patterns for establish ing a learning resources center on a community college campus. This chapter is an attempt to bring some of the loose ends together for sound planning. The reader should understand that he cannot take this plan and use it effectively in his own unique situation. "One conclusion we can make is that, as for college, university, public, and special library buildings, each junior college library building is a law unto itself, dependent on the community within which it is constructed and must exist for the guidelines which control its every feature. If there are any features which pertain to the junior college library alone, they have not yet been identified."[40]

Chapter IX

NEW TRENDS AND POSSIBLE EFFECTS

As the community college system develops, new as well as traditional ideas will become a part of institutional planning and structure. Many innovations, fostered by the administration and faculty, will lead to modifications in the nature of the services and instruction that the learning resources center provides. What will be the future role of the center? Will it be a traditional storehouse of and place for access to information? Will learning take place in the home or at the school, or perhaps in industry? Will there be widely used formats of knowledge other than books? Will the center need to provide more or less space for storage of materials?

It is the purpose of this chapter to explore and discuss trends and developments in materials, methods, and curricular organization that will affect the operation of the learning resources center within the next two decades. Examples of such trends are: variable entry and exit scheduling, television, the cassette versus dial access, the information explosion and microforms, audio-tutorial methods of instruction, the library-college concept, and computer services. Although many of these topics are interrelated, they will be discussed separately for the sake of clarity. Such trends should be examined to discover whether we are innovating for innovation's sake or to benefit the majority of students.

Variable Entry and Exit

The variable entry and exit scheduling allows students to enroll at any date during the semester, that is, all students do not have to register during the week prior to the beginning of the semester.

124

If on November 6 a student wants to begin college, this system allows him to start on that date.

This change in calendar structure is almost totally dependent upon a change in curricular structure—an individualized program for learning. The teacher fulfills an assisting and diagnostic role. He no longer lectures to groups and often his presentation is through locally prepared units of instruction via slides and cassettes or tapes. These units of instruction are frequently prepared utilizing behavioral objectives in the three domains. Students are not confined to time slots of 45 minutes to one hour duration three times a week for 3 hours credit but instead go to the classroom or laboratory as frequently as needed and stay as long as desired for the facility should be open and staffed approximately fifteen hours daily. Learning, therefore, is the total responsibility of the student and when the assignments for the course are completed and the objectives of the course are met, the student is ready to go to the next course or module whether or not he is at the end of the traditional semester. Thus the student is not confined to the semester or quarter calendar.

Such scheduling and individualized learning programs may cause many problems for the learning resources center. First, because of the heavy reliance upon behavioral objectives and media, a strong staff in terms of production and knowledge of instructional strategies is needed. Media personnel are in many cases asked to work with specific instructors in producing, testing and revising the materials. Often persons working in the audiovisual area are requested and want to become involved in writing or outlining objectives. Depending upon the prior experience of the instructor operating in this mode of instruction, the requests for the center's participation will vary considerably.

For an instructor who is contemplating working in this mode of instruction, planning, writing objectives, production, and investigating already produced materials should begin at least one year prior to the initial meeting of the class. Generally speaking, if the materials can be purchased and modified to meet the objectives, the institution will save money, and instructor's time can be better utilized, for local production is expensive. If enough time is not allotted for production, the audiovisual personnel and the faculty member often find that the pressures of working together vastly increase as the deadline date draws near.

The personnel needed and budget required to set up the variable entry and exit approach to curriculum are generally expensive. It is the responsibility of the learning resources director to make sure that the resources in the center are available in personnel and money. Without a strong commitment from the institution, the chances for failure are greatly enhanced. The money to support such a project does not greatly diminish once the project is on the road to success, for additional materials and equipment along with constant revisions are necessary and require time.

Often a question arises concerning the independent study approach and the utilization of the materials in the book format. If the objectives are written in such a manner, library utilization can and often increases. In courses not requiring special laboratory equipment, the learning experiences are placed in the library where the hardware is available and facilities are open for longer periods of time.

In summary, the variable entry and exit approach to curriculum structure is an asset to the student but an institutional commitment should be obtained before embarking upon major revisions in the curricula organization required.

*Audio-Tutorial Instruction**

A close ally of the variable entry and exit curricula is the audio-tutorial method of instruction. The audio-tutorial system of instruc-

*Auto and audio-tutorial are often used synonymously in literature. Whereas one generally is involving self instruction, the other one usually places more emphasis on sound through self instruction.

tion is a segment of the variable entry and exit in that the audio-tutorial method usually consists of a course or of several courses within a discipline. Scheduling with the mode of instruction is usually confined to the traditional semester or quarter system. Often the system consists of the following: an independent study session, a general assembly session, a small assembly session and other activities.[1] In many community colleges, the biology and health occupations have adopted this concept in varying degrees.

This system allows a modification of the student's behavior in allowing him to review or enlarge upon meaningful experiences established in the classroom. The student is allowed to strive to reach his greatest potential by active involvement at his own rate of development and the student who needs assistance may find materials on various tracks. Thus a student receives guided instruction, but he can also utilize as much time as needed through integrated books, slides, filmstrips, film loops, and video tapes. The system also

(1) Allows for independent study whereby a student may proceed at his own rate; thus the slow learner may repeat a lesson as needed;

(2) Introduces a student to a variety of learning experiences;

(3) Serves as a private tutor;

(4) Allows the absentee a chance to make up the missed work;

(5) Provides review exercises;

(6) Allows the student to isolate himself from the surrounding environment and to concentrate on the material to be studied;

(7) Provides an opportunity for the student to have the material at hand in a central location;

(8) Presents the subject matter in specific units so each student can proceed at his own rate;

(9)   Permits the student to learn when he is ready, not at a specific
time scheduled two months previously.

Because of the similarity to the variable entry and exit curriculum,
the audio-tutorial system has similar requirements for the learning
resources center. The audio-tutorial approach, as previously stated,
usually is not a campus wide activity and is offered in terms of the
traditional calendar. However, in production time and cost, problems can arise. As the project gets underway, more and more material
are required in duplicate, and duplication itself may become quite a
task. In some cases, a conflict of interest may occur in the center because of the time and support required by a few faculty members to
prepare materials as compared to the rest of the faculty. The audio-
tutorial projects are usually found in laboratories throughout the
campus and not in the learning resources center. Often outlays of
expensive hardware are necessary. For instance, the nursing department may need twelve carrels each equipped with tape recorder, 35
mm slide projector and 8 mm projector. If there are several programs
on campus, one can imagine the cost in hardware alone. Fortunately,
several programs may share the same facilities reducing the hardware outlay. It is recommended that enough materials and equipment be provided so that the laboratory can still function if one
set of materials is lost or there is failure of a piece of equipment.

The Library-College Concept
   The total osmosis of the library and instruction has been a dream
of the librarian for years, yet few have truly succeeded. As mentioned
throughout this book, service is not the total thrust of the learning
resources center, but a primary one. Traditionally, the library has
supported instruction; however, in the library-college concept the
library is absorbed into instruction and the total college. The library
is the college. Independent study, mediated instruction, seminars,
and flexibility run rampant. The librarian is a teacher (other than

library instruction) and the teacher is the librarian. There are few lectures but much dialogue. Teachers become students and students teachers and the institution is alive. Although the above is perhaps a dream on most campuses, many people are accepting the library-college movement and attempting to implement the concept.

Lee Lebbin lists the basic elements of the movement as follows: "(1) The learning mode is library-centered rather than classroom centered; (2) greater emphasis is placed on the process of learning than in memorization; (3) there is a joint student-faculty search and synthesis; (4) there is off-campus community service and field work; (5) there is greater emphasis on ideas and problems as the approach to subject matter rather than on geographic areas and periods of time; and (6) the faculty is essentially a cross between library-oriented teachers and teacher-oriented librarians."[2]

The purpose of the movement is to shift the emphasis from the physical classroom setting or teacher-telling to that of investigation and discussion assisted and managed by the group of fellow learners (both students and teachers). Then learning is self-initiated and motivation to learn comes through interaction with others and with the available resources. The academic lockstep is broken and the needs of the individual become paramount. Instead of fragmentation of the instructional program, there is a spirit of cooperativeness and unity as faculty, students, and administration lose their identity and work together as learners.

Needless to say, there is a tremendous slant toward the potential of human resources throughout the college and the learning resources center. Dedication to this philosophical viewpoint for learning is necessary in the selection of personnel and only through careful selection of personnel will this concept become a reality. The impact of this concept upon the learning resources center could make it truly the center of the college.[3]

Information Explosion—Information Retrieval and Microforms
    The information explosion is increasing the body of knowledge
with incredible speed. New developments confront us before we
understand and perhaps experience the old. Concerned parents and
teachers wonder what the impact of mass communication will have
on today's and tomorrow's children.

    If the accumulation of knowledge is plotted on a time line,
beginning with the birth of Christ, it is estimated that the first
doubling of knowledge occurred in 1750, the second in 1900,
the third in 1950, and the fourth only ten years later.[4]
    Scholars, faculty researchers, and graduate students are
drowning in a sea of data, and locating and obtaining any
specific item of information is becoming harder and more time
consuming . . . The library of the University of Illinois Chicago
Undergraduate Division, for example, will have to grow 1,000
percent in less than 10 years and is making preparation to do
so.[5]

    Knowledge is useless unless it can be effectively communicated.
The rapidity of change has made it next to impossible to assess
future needs; however, two things are certain—the need for access
to available knowledge, and the need for more effective storage
devices.
    The capabilities of random access stagger the imagination of any
professor contemplating research. It is currently impossible to know
whether or not one has exhausted the literature when searching for
a particular topic. Think of the ramifications of keying in certain
words and having a computer printout of all materials which are
applicable to the topic. Or even better yet, imagine the community
college library being tied into the large university library, the state
library and the public library, and being able to get quick and total
access to these resources.

Readily available random access is still in the future; however, as technology advances one must keep aware of its possibilities for the community college learning resources center in terms of the college itself and in terms of sharing resources through networks.

Microforms may be an answer to the access and storage problem. Because of their size they are easily shipped and stored: for example, the ERIC documents. The economy of storage of microfilm as compared to bound volumes is staggering since approximately five hundred reels of microfilm can be stored in the same space as 75 typical bound volumes. In microfiche, a 30,000 volume community college library can be stored in a small room, not 3,000 square feet. Other advantages of microreproductions include the following:

(1)   They are not as easily destroyed or damaged as printed book formats

(2)   They are somewhat inexpensive to purchase. Most fiche costs approximately one dollar compared to the cost of a book which may average $10.

(3)   The faculty member can have an index to the library materials in his office.

(4)   The possibility of duplicate libraries on branch campuses or in other areas of the college are attractive.

Some of the disadvantages of microforms include:

(1)   Much material is not currently available in microform.

(2)   Some students and faculty do not like to use material in microform because it does not feel like, nor is it as easily read as the printed physical volume.

(3)   Color reproductions are not up to par with printed materials, especially important for works of art.

There is little doubt at this time, that microforms are not widely accepted by students and faculty members in the community college. There has been a trend, however, for many libraries to begin purchasing duplicates of periodicals in microform to insure complete files. The newly established community college has to rely upon microforms for back issues of periodicals.

In conclusion, microforms are here to stay, and for libraries with low budgets, microforms may be a partial answer. In the next decade more and more materials will be available in microform and the micro-reader will become more convenient to utilize as the hardware is further perfected. Resistance to use of this format of materials will not change overnight but progress is being made. The learning resources center of the future will have to give more consideration to microforms in terms of planning, and the development of new facilities as well as changing utilization of old facilities.

Television

Television, other than commercial, is usually subdivided into two categories: educational and instructional. Instructional television is more narrow in scope and generally includes those activities which are direct instruction. For example, an explanation of a Shakespearean theater by an instructor over television is considered instructional while a drama performance from the college shown to the community citizenry is considered educational.

Within the next decade the advent of community cable television probably will become a reality in a majority of cities located in community college districts. Colleges may want to explore the possibility of having a channel or channels to utilize at the expense of the cable company. The possibilities in terms of educational opportunity and community service are great. All citizens of the district may be provided with a home learning center. The opportunities for reaching the district for inservice education, public opinion, formal educating, and selling the college to the community are im-

mense. For example, ninety-five per cent of families whose income qualified them for Office of Economic Opportunity assistance own at least one working black and white TV set.[6]
Typical utilization of television may be able

(1) To provide total direct instruction by locally produced programs or through rental sources such as Great Plains;
(2) To allow for guest lectures to be video taped for playback at a later time;
(3) To provide micro teaching units so that students may utilize video tapes on an individualized study basis;
(4) To allow many students to see a demonstration which perhaps is so small that normally only one person at a time may view;
(5) To provide students creative freedom to develop communicative skills through television medium (English, Drama, Speech);
(6) To teach the television medium to media, drama, journalism, and speech students;
*(7) To record commercial programs or segments of programs from commercial stations for discussion purposes;
*(8) To record films or segments of films for class discussion;
(9) To record instructors and students for self evaluation;
(10) To send college programming whether instructional, educational or recreational into the community homes via cable television.

Although there are many other possibilities, these are some which are more frequently utilized. Self contained portable video tape systems are already on many community college campuses in the ½ inch format and they have become almost commonplace with

*May infringe upon copyright laws.

the audiovisual facility. The video cassette is now on the market
and will be extensively utilized in the near future.

However, a separate television facility in which considerable studio
production will be taking place is a mistake unless it has the cooperation and support, particularly monetary, from the faculty, the Dean
of Instruction, and the President. The initial cost is only the first
and perhaps a minor consideration when viewing future expenditures. The cost required for releasing faculty to program, for a director and for the supportive personnel to operate the facility
can be staggering. Too often, the support of the faculty is not obtained, and they consider television another method used by administration to replace them, instead of a way to make instruction
more meaningful to the student.

In many cases, the addition of television to the audiovisual facility
as another function of the unit is wise and does not reach the mag-
nitude in cost and support as does the creation of a separate administrative unit. The director of the center, the dean, and the president
should plan the allocation of the educational budget to support
television. Because television is tied in with the instructional effort
of the college as a whole and also with the community service aspect, a simple solution such as the allocation of a few thousand
additional dollars to the learning resources center budget is not
sufficient. If this principle is followed, the book budget or materials
budget may suffer as the costs of television rise.

It is recommended that television be integrated with the audiovisual facility and that if colleges go beyond the simple aspects of
television they should form consortia. The future of television is
bright; however, each college should carefully analyze its potential.

Dial Access versus Cassettes

Five years ago, dial access systems were being installed in many
community colleges to increase student access to programmed
materials through audio and video tape. Thus, a student could

select and use an instructional program from a variety of campus locations by means of a dial or touch-tone buttons. One or two systems modified this concept so that audio presentations could be received in the home through telephone lines. Unfortunately, emphasis was too often placed on the acquisition of hardware instead of on producing adequate programs. Faculty members were not allowed sufficient released time to prepare and produce materials needed in order to use the system for instruction.

Technical inadequacies have also lessened the effectiveness of dial access systems. Most systems do not allow the user to stop and rewind and thus to utilize or review the program in small segments. An additional difficulty has been the need to make a program available to more than one student at a time. A user's choice was often either to wait until his selection was available or to dial into it in progress.

This early pioneering of dial access systems, however, has reinforced the concept that hardware is useless unless proper software is developed and faculty support obtained. Such systems have also allowed greater experimentation with making the home the center of learning.

Currently, the use of audio cassettes has met with considerable success. Instead of a program being restricted to a single tape in a dial access system, cassettes can be duplicated and supplied to students at a minimal cost. They can be mailed to students or checked out of the learning resources center as a book. Cassette players allow the student to proceed slowly through a lesson and listen to small segments when necessary. Hardware cost and maintenance is greatly reduced when compared to dial access. The cassette has slowed the trend of dial access for the present. Changes are anticipated, however, in both areas so that the home becomes a learning center, and students are not tied to the campus for completion of assignments.

Library Application of Computer Services

The computer offers vast potential for the areas of circulation, technical services and ordering, and book lists or reproductions of the card catalog. The current system of operation must be analyzed in terms of whether it is meeting the required tasks and how efficiently. Such internal analysis, if successfully completed, may so greatly enhance the operation of the facility that the computer will not be needed. The computer is not a cure all and generally speaking it can increase inflexibility within the operation. "Almost everyone who has computerized will confess, if pushed, that any real savings are as yet unrealized, though still hoped for in the future."[7]

There are several considerations to be analyzed: What is the size of the student population; what is the projected enrollment for the next decade; are the policies of loaning materials stabilized; is the learning resources center willing to rely upon computer services rather than its staff for control of data and records; will a computer require additional personnel or additional capital outlay?

In the circulation area, the records and posting of overdue notices can be completed routinely by computer. But in the community college setting how many part-time students do not have their identification cards when needed? Is the reserve book section to be computerized although books may be checked out for 1 hour, 2 hours, 3 days and other calendar variations? One final consideration is that, if it is not possible to go "on line," is it possible to wait for a day to receive the reports from computer services?

In the areas of technical services and acquisition one question should be immediately asked—is the budget and the numbers of volumes processed of such a large size that it is worthwhile to computerize?

In starting a new community college library, holdings should certainly be listed on a computer if one is available. If the library inputs the call number, author, title, publisher and other necessary information (to be determined by each library) the library can print a list of holdings for each faculty member by running the list on ditto stencil and duplicating the necessary copies. In this manner cost is reduced for a book catalog, and each faculty member may have a copy of the library's holdings at a minimal cost. This, however, is not a replacement of a conventional card catalog.

Without doubt, the computer will play an increasingly important role in information dissemination in the community college and in our daily lives. However, each community college must determine what is needed that cannot be accomplished without the computer. Will the end product justify the means and cost? There are still a lot of unanswered questions as to the applications and feasibility of the computer for a medium and large community college learning resources center.

Summary

There are many new trends in ideas and materials which may change the nature of the learning resources center. Perhaps the most noticeable changes will occur with changes in curriculum structure. The interests and convenience of the student may become a primary factor in designing learning experiences, and learning itself may take place outside the confines of the institution. The curriculum may become individualized so that students can learn what they want to learn when they want to learn. It is the responsibility of the center to be responsive to change.

Chapter X

SUMMARY AND RECOMMENDATIONS

The purpose of this investigation has been to develop a rationale for a learning resources center within the community college. To date, few comprehensive plans have been published which give direction in establishing and maintaining a center on the community college campus. Therefore, an attempt has been made to review relevant research in the fields of library science and audiovisual education and to integrate these findings into a workable plan to be used as a guide. The nature of the community college; its philosophy and organization; its administration and personnel requirements; finance; the selection of materials and equipment; instructional and technical services; the library technical assistant; and a building program for new facilities are some of the subjects considered.

It is the purpose of this chapter to summarize the findings and to report recommendations for utilization.

The Nature of the Community College

Less costly, lower division, continuing, and post-secondary education is now available in many states for students from various backgrounds in the community colleges recently established throughout the United States. The community college concept has become a national development. In 1970 community colleges enrolled approximately two million students. The rapid rise in enrollment appears to have stemmed from two sources: the increase in population, and the demands and aspirations of American society.

The rapid increase in establishing community colleges is necessary to accommodate our changing society, but techniques and practices must not and cannot be adapted in whole from secondary or from four-year institutions. The community college movement should evolve its own philosophy and techniques and not be burdened by the traditionalism of other educational institutions for the community college has developed in our country to fulfill particular needs.

Community college students may be described in terms of widely varying aptitudes, socio-economic backgrounds, marital status, and age. The student population is generally comprised of two distinct age groups, those from eighteen to twenty-one, and those students who are not classified as of college age. In many cases community college students have been found lower in academic potential, and they have selected their institution for practical reasons of proximity and cost.

Because of the diverse backgrounds and the interests of the community college student population, the curricula must be appropriately diversified and relevant to the interests, abilities, and goals of the student. The curricula also must be sensitive to local manpower needs and the social and cultural interests of the area. The responsibility for initiating and maintaining a comprehensive curriculum rests primarily with the faculty and administration, working through the curriculum council and advisory committees. The community college must commit itself to continuous self-examination, experimentation, and communication both within the institutional system and with the students.

The faculty in community colleges may have as diverse backgrounds as the students they instruct. They range in experience and education from those with doctorates to those with no degrees, and have extensive experience or no experience.

The typical junior college faculty member is an individual who has adequate-to-superior preparation, and personal perception of the middle and upper-lower class. The teachers who stand out among their peers have two characteristics in common: they are keenly and obviously interested in and enthusiastic about their subject matter, and they are thoroughly prepared.

The Philosophy and Organization

The traditional library is disappearing along with separate facilities for library and audiovisual activities. Combined library and audiovisual services are not always harmonious within institutions, but they must become so if the community colleges are to meet the needs of the students and faculty within a changing environment. The students are living in a complex and media-oriented society and no one particular format for communication can be considered as the one best for all. When print and non-print materials and services are coordinated into one center, under one objective, they are more accessible, providing greater potential for use and greater potential for learning. A recent survey of community colleges indicated that three-fourths were currently administering the library and audiovisual services as a single unit. Guidelines are being modified and rewritten to reflect the unified media concept.

Instructional practices in modern education do not entail a conflict between new media and printed materials. It is the purpose of the learning resources center to mold together the various media in a systematic pattern and put at the disposal of the students and teaching faculty the effective communication of ideas through services and technology.

The enrollment and scope of services to be implemented by the learning resources center will affect the organization of the administrative unit. The problems involved in administrating the unit, regardless of its size, will be of a nature that will require training and experience in library, audiovisual, curriculum, and management areas.

The most common organizational pattern for the learning resources center with an enrollment of 5,000 full-time equivalent has a director of the center who is responsible to the dean of instruction or vice president in charge of instruction. Occasionally, the director will be responsible to the president. The director has under his direct supervision, a coordinator of library services who has as his responsibility the operation of the library, and a coordinator of audiovisual services who is responsible for the audiovisual operations. The two coordinators should have formal training and experience in both the library and audiovisual areas.

The training of audiovisual and library technicians has been instituted in over one hundred community colleges in the United States. The responsibilities of initiating and administering these programs should fall within the realm of the dean of instruction and be delegated to the director of the learning resources center.

The philosophy of the center should be two-fold: (1) the servicing of faculty and student needs, and (2) the stimulation of faculty and students in integrating individualized instruction within the college curriculum. Through this administrative unit, excellence in service and instruction should be provided.

Administration and Personnel Requirements

The efficiency and accomplishment obtained by a learning resources center in meeting its desired educational goals will be reflected in the quality of staff it employs and the internal and external communication system that is established throughout the organization. To achieve the objectives requires the cooperation of each employee within the system. Each person must feel his individual worth and grow intellectually and emotionally. The success of the organization is achieved in terms of the role of each individual who participates and his perception of himself in this role.

Communication channels are important to the learning resources center personnel. The channels should not only flow downward but upward and horizontally. The lack of trust can keep subordinates from communicating with their supervisors and thereby inhibit the communication process. All personnel, professional, technical, and clerical should be involved in general functions such as planning, appraising, communicating, advising, and educating.

We must never assume that we are fully aware of what we communicate to someone else. There are tremendous distortions in meaning as men try to communicate with one another. The job of achieving understanding and insight into mental processes of others is much more difficult and the situation more serious than most of us care to admit.

The learning resources center should have a broadly educated and well qualified staff in the communication area. These positions will require familiarity with both print and non-print media and their implications and effectiveness in the process of communication.

There are no established requirements for professional training or experience for the director of a community college learning resources center. This position is usually filled by a person from the library field since most administrations still think of the library as a necessary but traditional fixture on the college campus. The director should have formal training in both library and audiovisual fields and have experience in both areas. The director should be a leader and a communicator with knowledge of the fields of curriculum theory, communication, library, audiovisual, and learning theory. He should know how to work with others and gain their respect.

The staff of the learning resources center can be divided into two categories: (1) the professional staff; and (2) the supportive staff.

The professional staff includes those employees who have advanced degrees in library and audiovisual fields, have considerable responsibility, understand the objectives of the learning resources center and the college, and understand the functions and operation of the center.

The supportive staff would consist of technicians and clerks. The formal training of the technicians in library and audiovisual techniques will vary from college to college; however, they should have some formal training and experience in the technical aspects of learning resource center duties and responsibilities. In the absence of formal training and experience, on-the-job training is a must.

The clerks can be of tremendous assistance to the professional and technical staff. They should be carefully supervised by professional staff and should be consulted relative to the operation of basic objectives of the center.

The effective center will integrate all elements into cohesive units and success will come when each person realizes that he does not have a specific position but a responsibility, and in fulfilling this responsibility, strives for excellence.

Finance

When the library and audiovisual are unified into one administrative unit, it is logical that a unified budget and the distribution of the budget should be under the control of the director of the learning resources center. If the director is going to successfully prepare and administer the budget, he should be aware of the budgeting process of the parent institution.

The director's relationship with the dean of business or business manager should include the following: preparation of purchase orders, approval for payment of invoices, checking business manager's monthly accounts against the center's records, inventory of equipment, employment of non-professional help, transfer of funds from one budget category to another, approval of payroll for student employees, and approval of major repairs and renovation of the building and equipment.

The business manager should expect the director to make purchases within the prescribed budget, route all purchase requisitions through the business office unless the director is authorized to issue and sign purchase orders directly to dealers and publishers, and to forward, with the director's approval, invoices to the business office promptly for payment. The business manager expects the director to use the appropriations wisely and to give an exact accounting of the funds he administers.

Budgeting is a means of planning for efficiency and economy. It should be planned for the present and future since it is the fiscal interpretation of the center's program.

Important areas to be considered in planning a budget are: (1) what accrediting agency standards are involved; (2) what percentage of the total institutional budget is to be allocated to the learning resources center; (3) is the center in the "establishing" period or in the "established" period; (4) are funds to be allocated on a dollar basis for each department within the institution, or will the director allocate purchases only when specifically requested by individual faculty and students?

Depending upon the philosophy of the institution and the services provided, six to ten per cent of the educational budget should be allocated to the learning resources center. If it is in the "establishing" period more funds are usually necessary.

The book fund, next to salaries, is usually the largest item in the budget. This fund is usually administered in one of two ways: (1) the funds are administered directly by the director to whom all requests are made by faculty members when they wish to order books and materials; (2) the funds are distributed in fixed amounts for the needs of each of the teaching departments.

The size of the budget inevitably determines to a large extent the scope and effectiveness of the center's program. The present holdings, type of college served, size of faculty and students, variety and spread of subject fields covered, and extent to which the college encourages the use of supplementary materials in various formats are factors which influence budgetary needs.

Comparisons of expenditures of one college with another should be avoided because of local conditions including assessed valuation, size of enrollment, curriculum offered, progress stages of the development of the center, and the objectives of the center.

The success of the center in financial matters will depend upon the allocation of the budget and the manner in which these finances are administered.

Selection of Materials and Equipment

Proper techniques and sound judgment of the institution's personnel must be utilized in the selection of equipment and materials if the institution can truthfully boast of an adequate collection which meets the needs of the faculty and students and meets the educational objectives of the institution.

The director of the learning resources center assumes the fiscal responsibility for the selection process. He may not be immediately involved in the actual selection; however, it is his responsibility to coordinate the selection policies with the educational objectives of the college.

The selection of materials should be influenced by the following factors: (1) size of the institution; (2) educational objectives of the institution; (3) scope of the curriculum; (4) size of the current collection; (5) adequacy of collection; and (6) funds which are currently available.

The community college has the selection problems of both the liberal arts college and the vocational training institution because it is a combination of both and is usually offering both types of curricula. At the same time it is required to provide materials for leisure activities and non-credit adult education classes.

The primary purpose of equipment and materials selection is to develop a complete and comprehensive collection as measured by utilization. Most standards established by accrediting agencies are quantitative in nature instead of qualitative. Basic number of volumes per institution and books per pupil should not be a determining factor in building an adequate collection of equipment and materials.

The trend in academic libraries has been toward selection by library personnel rather than faculty. Selection should be the joint responsibility of the teaching staff and learning resources center staff. Often those assuming selection responsibilities are guided by budget allocations.

The vocational area is a major element of the total curricula and purchases and allotments of funds for new programs should be seriously studied. The selection of materials for this area is often a problem because of: (1) number and variety of technical-vocational programs; (2) orientation of the learning resources personnel; (3) lack of published selection guides; (4) lack of available materials in recently developed areas.

The number of magazines needed for a community college is also controversial among learning resources center personnel and accrediting agencies. Again, numbers should not be the major criteria, but rather the needs of the institution to support the educational objectives should be the prime consideration.

There are many selection aids that can be effectively used by learning resources center personnel and faculty. Some of the guides are as follows: (1) *Choice*; (2) *Books for College Libraries*; (3) *Book for Junior Colleges*; (4) *The Junior College Library Collection*; (5) *A Basic Book Collection for the Community College*; (6) *The Julian Street List*; (7) *Publisher's Weekly*; (8) *Library Journal*; (9) *New York Times Book Review*; (10) *Books in Print*; (11) *Reader's Advisor*; (12) *The NICEM directories*; (13) *National Audio Tape Catalog*; and (14) *Audiovisual Equipment Directory*.

A well balanced collection does not happen by chance and adequacy should be measured according to the objectives of the institution.

Instructional and Technical Services

The many services provided by the learning resources center could well be divided into two areas: instructional and technical.

Two important decisions must be determined relative to the instructional services: (1) to whom should the services be given; (2) what will be the nature of the services?

There is little, if any, doubt about the center serving the students, faculty, and administration on the college campus. A major question to be decided is: should the center provide services to all citizens of the community college district? Since the community college district is comprised of and supported by the citizens within the district, it should be assumed that services will be provided for all citizens of the college district. The types and extent of services should be determined by each individual district.

The nature of the services will vary from institution to institution. How the Learning Resources Center will sell its services to faculty and students is an important question. Knowledge of the utilization requirements of faculty and students must be obtained before the center can effectively administer a good program. One method of determining the utilization requirement is through student and faculty surveys. An analysis of such surveys indicates that students tend to use materials because they are required to use them, and that the majority of students utilize their own materials and not the center's when studying in the learning resources center.

The technical services area is responsible for the ordering of magazines, books, and other print and non-print materials, checking invoices against purchase orders, accounting of funds allocated to the department, cataloging and classifying materials, filing catalog cards, and other processing techniques that may be required to make materials available for student and faculty use. The department should be organized in a manner to allow a work flow beginning with the ordering process to the finished product for patron usage. Utilization may be increased through interfiling print and non-print materials in the card catalog.

Automation is receiving increased attention. Increasing costs of services, and the emphasis upon professional personnel doing professional duties, are factors related to automation. The learning resources center, particularly technical services, has a responsibility to keep informed as to what changes automation can bring to the department and to the center. It is the duty of technical services to serve as liaison and through its specialized knowledge help plan automation systems for the center.

The Library Technical Assistant

There has not been complete agreement among professional librarians as to the need for formal college training for middle range personnel performing duties on a level between the professional and clerical ranges. Some library authorities have encouraged the establishment of a library technology program to train library technicians to work under the supervision of a professional librarian and to relieve the professional from duties that do not require full professional training. The library technology programs now in progress are offered in over one hundred community colleges across the nation. The semester hours offered in library and audiovisual vary with the institution ranging from six to thirty semester hours in the two-year programs.

The library and information fields are concerned with the availability of trained manpower at every level and in every type of library and information center. Results of recent studies indicate a large and increasing need for library technical assistants and library clerks.

Research indicates that those institutions serving relatively large community areas seemed to be most successful in establishing their training programs and placing their graduates, and the highest salaries offered are in special or industrial libraries. Greater responsibility is placed upon the technician in smaller libraries, especially the school and public libraries. There is considerable disagreement between the employee and employer when answers were given concerning beginning salary levels and the acceptance of the library technician as a bona fide library worker by professional staff.

There is strong evidence to indicate that the formal training of library technical assistants will be delegated to the community college because it is a two-year vocational oriented program and not a four-year academic college program. The tendencies of employers to accept library technical assistants will increase as a standardized program of course work is accepted by institutions offering the program. To date, each community college offering the program has developed its own courses of study and requirements for certificate and graduation.

A Building Program for New Facilities

One of the major efforts in the building program of a new campus is the design and development of a functional learning resources center. The size of the maximum projected enrollment should help to determine the size and design of the facilities. Items such as furniture and interiors should be considered separately. The planning should include representation of the institution's administration, the director of learning resources center, consultants, architects, board members, faculty and students. They may not all be involved specifically in details, but they should help determine major considerations which affect the building program. The director has the responsibility to collect data from many inputs and coordinate these with the architects into a building plan.

Each area for the learning resources center must be carefully planned to secure the greatest possible economy and efficiency. The reading room, carrels, listening and viewing rooms, book stacks, offices, conference rooms, work rooms, and storage areas must all be planned to meet immediate and future needs.

No one philosophy can be established for all community colleges since it varies with each institution. It is important to determine the philosophy of the institution and the relationship of the learning resources center to the total instructional effort before planning becomes specific. The materials and physical features should provide for differences in tastes, abilities, and needs; offering a wide range of materials and providing spaces for quiet individual research, group study, listening, viewing and recreational reading.

The building must be arranged for effective economical operation and must have an attractive, informal, orderly appearance in order to develop in its patrons an appreciation and enjoyment of its materials and services and to fulfill the objectives of the college. The building must allow for expansion and change with few structural modifications.

A spatial relationship diagram of the library functions of the center should include the following areas: lobby, offices, circulation area, periodical area, technical services, card catalog, reference area, reading and study areas, stacks, faculty reading area, typing facilities for students, microfilm and magazine storage areas, group study facilities, and receiving and storage.

A spatial relationship diagram of the audiovisual facilities should include the following: lobby, reception and scheduling, storage and repair, graphics and production, television studios and control rooms, listening stations, basic skills laboratory, preview rooms, recording studios, and dark rooms.

The space allocated for housing the learning resources center will be based upon standards within the library and audiovisual fields, the amount of money available for a building program, and the relationship of the learning resources center to the educational method and objectives of the college.

The advantages of different floor coverings and acoustics need careful study and consideration. The library technology project of the American Library Association has done considerable research in this area and their findings should be studied.

In the next decade vast changes will occur in information distribution within the community college campus. Automated circulation, bibliographic control, mechanization of technical services, "wet" carrels, television distribution, and computer assisted instruction are some examples of progress currently being accomplished. The building should be planned so that innovations can be made with a minimum of structural changes and costs.

Innovation: New Trends and Possible Effects

As the college develops and pursues its educational goals, new methods and techniques of instruction will be utilized. These developments may modify the nature of service that the center will provide. It may even change its role to the extent that the center as we know it today may disappear in the structure of the college; that is, all learning will not take place in the classroom as all research will not take place in the library.

Variable entry and exit scheduling allows students to enroll anytime during the calendar year. If the student decides that today is the day to begin college he may enroll. Each program is individualized, and the instructor fulfills an assisting and diagnostic role. Learning becomes the total responsibility of the student and "institutional time" is not a factor to hinder learning. The personnel of the center will become deeply involved in working with faculty to support their curricular needs in both hardware and software.

The audio-tutorial method of instruction is similar to variable entry and exit. Audio-tutorial systems are currently being offered during the traditional calendar. Generally the most common organization of the course is for large group, small group, and independent study sessions. The student is allowed to pursue guided instruction at his own rate through integrated media during the independent study sessions. This system also places a greater emphasis of monetary and personnel support from the learning resources center to instruction.

The Library College Concept concentrates its effort in absorbing the library into the college. The learning mode of the institution becomes library centered rather than classroom centered. Learning becomes self-initiated, and the motivation to learn comes through inter action with others in the academic community. In this movement faculty, students, and administration lose their identity and all work together as learners.

The impact of rapidly increasing numbers of materials is a problem which will continue to plague librarians. Currently, with the doubling of man's knowledge in recorded form taking less than ten years, new methods for storage and retrieval are necessary. Although microform are not at the present as widely accepted as the hardcover format of media by the user, libraries are going to find it necessary to purchase and utilize microforms along with emphasis on integration in informa tion retrieval systems for the future.

The computer offers vast potential for the learning resources center in its daily operations. Along with completing daily routines, the facility can and will play an increasingly important role in dissemination of information. The costs of computer applications to the library are high; however, colleges, especially the smaller community college should begin to plan to develop consortia to maximize resources and reduce cost if computer applications are seriously considered.

The cassette at present has almost replaced the earlier trend toward installation of dial access systems in community colleges. The cassette is cheaper and provides more flexibility than the expensive and complex installation of the dial access system. The video cassette may expand the opportunities and alternatives now available with the audio cassette. There is little doubt that economical retrieval systems will be developed in the near future so that programs originating in the community college will be available in the home.

In the next decade community cable television systems will become a reality. This will enable the college to take the campus into the home. Currently many colleges are effectively utilizing portable self-contained television systems in a multitude of ways throughout the campus. However, equipping and maintaining a comprehensive television facility should be well planned based on its projected use in the curriculum, and colleges, whenever possible, should seek cooperative ventures with neighboring colleges for maximum use of facilities.

Recommendations

1. The community college should commit itself to continuous self evaluation, experimentation, and communication both within the institutional system and with the students. The community college should develop its learning resources center based on the needs of the individual institution rather than following the patterns of high schools or college or university libraries.

2. The learning resources center serving an institution of 5,000 full-time-equivalent students should combine the library and audiovisual departments into one media center. The administration should employ a director who has formal training and experience in the following areas: library, audiovisual, curriculum, a teaching field, and one who has knowledge and experience in the areas of management and administration.

3. The director should be responsible for employing his supportive personnel. He should have the authority to delegate responsibilities and duties to professional, technical, and clerical staff. The director should employ coordinators in charge of library and audiovisual areas. They in turn are to be responsible for supervision of staff in their respective areas. The coordinators should report directly to the director of the center.

4. There should be a unified budget for the center. The coordinators should help the director in preparation of the budget, in controlling the expenditures within their respective areas, and in conforming with the approved budgeted items in their departments.

The director's responsibilities should include originating and signing purchase orders that involve books, materials, and supplies. Purchases of capital outlay items should be approved by the director and business office. All invoices should be approved by the coordinators and director before presentation to the business office for payment. A minimum of 7 per cent of the total educational budget should be allocated for the learning resources center after the "establishing" period is over and more than 7 per cent should be allowed during the "establishing" period.

5. The selection of materials should be a joint responsibility of the learning resources center and faculty members. The control of the budget for books, materials, supplies, and equipment should remain with the director of the learning resources center and not be distributed to academic departments within the institution for their control.

The selection of materials should be qualitative and not quantitative for quantity has little meaning for the diversity of the curriculum offered in a community college. Quality is paramount in supporting the teaching staff and student.

6. The nature of technical services will vary from institution to institution. This department should be given responsibility, under the direction of the coordinator, for ordering magazines, books, and other print and non-print materials, checking invoices against purchase orders, accounting of funds allocated to the department, cataloging and classification of materials, filing of catalog cards, and other processing techniques required to make materials available for use. The card catalog should be divided and organized into three areas: (1) author; (2) title; and (3) subject.

7. In addition to the director of the learning resources center and the two coordinators, each major department should be staffed with professional employees and supportive staff consisting of library technical assistants, secretary-typists, and clerical employees.

8. Library technical assistants should be employed as supportive

staff to the professional staff. The technical assistant can be one who has had library courses in a two or four-year institution but does not have a four-year degree, or can be a four-year college degree person with library science courses or without library science courses. The employment of technicians will relieve the professional employees for duties that require a professional.

9. The director of the learning resources center, together with the administration and architects, should plan the learning resources facilities. The inputs of faculty and students should be seriously considered. The director should be given the responsibility for space planning of student and faculty areas, selection of furniture and equipment, and the arrangement of facilities for efficient economical operation. The director should also be aware of the changes which are occurring in information distribution and plan the space allocations so innovations can be added with very few structural changes in the building.

10. Institutions should form consortia whenever possible in order not to duplicate special collections. They should also pool resources when developing areas in which large capital expenditures and heavy financial support will be necessary, for example television.

Appendix A

Director of Learning Resources Center

The director of learning resources is directly responsible to the dean of instruction for the administration of the learning resources center. He is responsible for the library, audiovisual services, and self-instructional laboratory.

Some of the specific duties of the director are to:

1. Develop and maintain goals and objectives of the center which are in harmony with the institution.
2. Supervise and coordinate library functions and audiovisual services.
3. Assist in the selection, and be responsible for the supervision, of professional and support personnel. These responsibilities may be delegated to the coordinators of library and audiovisual areas respectively.
4. Establish and maintain communications between center personnel and the faculty and administration.
5. Be responsible for the development of library instruction for all freshmen with the cooperation of the division chairman of communications.
6. Plan and conduct pre-service and in-service training programs for center personnel and faculty.
7. Assist in the evaluation of center personnel and the services provided.
8. Assist the administration and architects in the planning and developing of physical facilities for the learning resources center and related areas such as language laboratories, large group instruction facilities, and independent study areas.
9. Recommend center policies and procedures.
10. Interpret college policy for center personnel.
11. Prepare budget and control expenditures.
12. Be responsible for the preparation and submission of appropriate college reports and documents.

13. Establish and maintain cooperative working relationships for faculty and students with public and private libraries in the college district.
14. Supervise the use and maintenance of equipment assigned to the center, including large group instruction facilities and language laboratories.
15. Be responsible for the library and audiovisual technician curricula including courses and personnel.
16. Support and maintain alternative methods of instruction through the center.
17. Continually review and assess the capabilities of television in the college and the community.
18. Report newsworthy activities occurring within the center for appropriate publicity.
19. Attend state and national meetings relating directly to the learning resources center objectives.

Coordinator of Audiovisual

The primary role of this position will be promoting mediated instruction. He will be in charge of the audiovisual area. He will serve as liason between the faculty and technicians in producing appropriate materials for instruction. He will be directly responsible to the director of learning resources.

His duties will consist of the following:

1. Assist the faculty in selection, evaluation, and purchase of commercially made material.
2. Assist the faculty in the effective utilization of materials.
3. Implement and develop mediated instruction into the most appropriate curricular designs.
4. Assist, when requested, faculty and administration in audiovisual presentations on and off campus.
5. Supervise the personnel including student help in the audiovisual area.
6. Conduct inservice instruction on production of materials and operation of equipment.
7. Assist faculty in the audio-tutorial laboratories with equipment and materials when necessary and requested.
8. Distribute and maintain all audiovisual equipment and supplies including equipment inventory.
9. Maintain reports on utilization and submit an annual report in the audiovisual area.
10. Maintain a system of ordering, distributing, and returning all rental and free educational films.
11. Prepare the budget and control expenditures in the audiovisual area.
12. See that commercially purchased materials are cataloged.
13. Maintain and operate all television and lecture hall systems.
14. Assist the director and assume any additional responsibilities he may delegate.

Coordinator of Libraries

The primary role of this position will be the library operation of the learning resources center. He will be directly responsible to the director of learning resources.

His duties will consist of the following:

1. Be responsible for the supervision of all personnel in the library area, including professional librarians, technical assistants and clerical personnel.
2. Coordinate all intradepartmental operations and delegate responsibilities to personnel in each department and establish their priorities, including circulation, technical processes, reference, and acquisitions and serials.
3. Be responsible for the acquisition and cataloging of all library materials.
4. Collect data and prepare all reports pertinent to the library area.
5. Coordinate the library instruction program.
6. Evaluate and make recommendations for the acquisition of gifts.
7. Establish and maintain cooperative working relationships for faculty and students with public and private libraries in the college district.
8. Coordinate the reference area and the preparation of bibliographies.
9. Create and maintain the vertical file.
10. Maintain and revise, when necessary, the library procedures handbook.
11. Assist in publicity efforts of the college through the director—including faculty guide, student guide, etc.
12. Assist in the preparation of the budget and control expenditures in the library area.
13. Promote the utilization of the library resources with faculty.
14. Conduct inventory as needed.
15. Assist the director and assume any additional responsibilities he may delegate.

Appendix B

BUDGET—LRC

Waubonsee Community College
1972-73*

120-000-511, 512	Administrator's and Librarians' salaries	64,500
516	Secretary-clerical salaries	23,100
518	Student salaries	4,000
532	Consultants' fees	200
534	Equipment repair	1,800
539	Services	2,500
120-000-542	Printing	300
543	Consumable supplies	14,000
544.01	Filmstrips, slides, etc. (commercially prepared)	6,300
544.02	Film rental	3,600
545.01	Library books and cards	35,000
545.02	Periodicals	4,600
546	Membership dues	200
120-000-552	Local travel	200
553	Convention travel	700
120-000-562	Rental of equipment	200
120-000-586	New Equipment	9,800
120-000-590	Other	100
120-000-600	Contingency	1,000

LEARNING RESOURCES CENTER TOTAL $172,100

---

*Based upon 1,650 FTE students.

Appendix C

Illinois Central College
Library Technology Program
Associate in Applied Science Degree

Freshman Year

Fall Semester		Credit Hours
LIB	110 Introduction to Libraries	3
LIB	120 Audiovisual I	3
ENGL	110 Composition	
or	111 Composition	3
*SECTR	110 Beginning Typing	4
	Laboratory Science	4
		17

Spring Semester		Credit Hours
LIB	115 Materials Selection	3
LIB	125 Cataloging and Classification	3
ENGL	111 Composition	
or	112 20th Century Topics	3
PSY	110 Introduction to Psychology	3
	Humanities	3
		15

*An elective will be substituted if the student is successful on a proficiency test administered by Illinois Central College.

Sophomore Year

Fall Semester	Credit Hours
LIB 210 Reference	3
HIST 111 World Civilization	4
Mathematics	3
Social Science	3
Electives	3
	16

Spring Semester	Credit Hours
LIB 230 Library Administration	3
LIB 240 Problems & Procedures of Circulation and Acquisition	3
LIB 220 Audiovisual II	3
Electives	8
	17

Electives

L 225 Photograph & Darkroom Techniques	3

Thornton Community College
Educational Media Technician
Associate Degree

		Credit Hrs.
First	Introduction to Educational Media	2
Semester	Educational Media Production Techniques	3
	Introduction to Photography	2
	Composition and Rhetoric	3
	Two-Dimensional Design	2
	Mathematics or Science Elective	3-4
	Physical Education	1
		16-17
Second	Educational Media Systems	2
Semester	Principles of Multi Media Presentation	3
	Special Techniques of Photography Production	2
	Advertising Design	2
	English Elective	3
	General Elective	3
	Physical Education	1
		16
Third	Television Production	3
Semester	Practicum I (Supervised Practice)	3
	Introduction to Electronics	3
	Social or Behavioral Science Elective	3
	General Elective	3
	Physical Education	1
		16

		Credit Hrs.
Fourth	Practicum II (Supervised Practice)	3
Semester	Introduction to Graphic Arts	3
	Introduction to Data Processing	3
	Fundamentals of Speech	3
	Social or Behavioral Science	3
	Physical Education	1
		16
	TOTAL FOR DEGREE	64-66

Thornton Community College

Educational Media Technician
Certificate Curriculum

		Credit Hrs.
First	Introduction to Educational Media	2
Semester	Educational Media Production Techniques . . .	3
	Introduction to Photography	2
	Two-Dimensional Design	2
	General Education Elective	3
		12
Second	Educational Media Systems	2
Semester	Principles of Multi-Media Presentation	3
	Introduction to Graphic Arts	3
	Special Techniques of Photographic	
	Production	2
	Advertising Design	2
		12
Third	Television Production	3
Semester	Practicum I (Supervised Practice)	3
	Introduction to Electronics	3
	General Education Elective	3
		12
	TOTAL FOR CERTIFICATE	36

Notes

Notes to Chapter I

1. American Association of Junior Colleges, *Junior Colleges in 50 States/50 Years* (Washington, D.C.: American Association of Junior Colleges, 1969).
2. Illinois Revised Statutes, *Illinois Public Junior College Act*, Chapter 122: Sections 101-111 to 108-112, 1969.
3. Illinois Junior College Board, *Report of Selected Data and Characteristics: Illinois Public Junior Colleges, 1970-71* (Springfield: Illinois Junior College Board, 1971), p. 5.
4. American Association of Junior Colleges, *1972 Junior College Directory* (Washington, D.C.: American Association of Junior Colleges, 1972), p. 7.
5. Edmund Gleazer, *This is the Community College* (Boston: Houghton Mifflin, 1968), p. 20.
6. James W. Thornton, *The Community Junior College* (New York: John Wiley, 1966), p. 287.
7. Leland L. Medsker, *The Junior College: Progress and Prospect* (New York: McGraw-Hill Book Company, 1960), pp. 43-45.
8. The American College Testing Program, Inc., *The Two-Year College and Its Students: An Empirical Report* (Iowa City, Iowa: The Corporation, 1969), pp. 42-46.
9. Clyde E. Blocker, Robert H. Plummer, and Richard C. Richardson, Jr., *The Two-Year College: A Social Synthesis* (Englewood Cliffs, N.J.: Prentice-Hall, 1965), pp. 240-241.
10. Patricia Cross, *The Junior College Student: A Research Description* (Princeton, New Jersey: Educational Testing Service, 1968), pp. 47-51.
11. The American College Testing Program, Inc., *The Two-Year College and Its Students: An Empirical Report,* p. 66.
12. Earl C. Kelley, "The Fully Functioning Self," *Perceiving, Behaving, Becoming: A New Focus* (Washington, D.C.: National Education Association, 1962), pp. 17-21.
13. Blocker, Plummer, and Richardson, pp. 118-120.
14. Noel F. McInnis, "Students Are a Lot Like People," *Junior College Journal,* XXXIX (March, 1968), pp. 40-44.
15. Illinois Revised Statutes, *Illinois Public Junior College Act,* Chapter 122:103-117, p. 225.
16. B. Lamar Johnson, "Needed: Experimental Junior Colleges," *Junior College Journal,* XXXVI (October, 1965), p. 20.
17. Gleazer, pp. 116-117.
18. Blocker, Plummer, and Richardson, p. 134.
19. National Education Association, Research Division, *Teacher Supply and Demand in Universities, Colleges, and Junior Colleges, 1963-64 and 1964-65* (Washington, D. C.: National Education Association, 1965), pp. 1-20.

20. Medsker, p. 172.
21. Arthur M. Cohen and Florence B. Brower, *Confronting Identity: The Community College Instructor* (Englewood Cliffs, New Jersey: Prentice-Hall, Inc., 1972), p. 220.
22. Blocker, Plummer, and Richardson, p. 138.
23. Win Kelly and Leslie Wilbur, *Teaching in the Community Junior College* (New York: Appleton-Century-Crofts, 1970), pp. 136-137.

Notes to Chapter II

1. Illinois Library Association, *A Multimedia Survey of Community College Libraries of the State of Illinois* (Chicago: Illinois Library Association, 1970), p. 1.
2. Ibid., p. 10.
3. Louis Shores, "The Library Junior College," *Junior College Journal*, XXXVI (March, 1966), p. 7.
4. William Miller, "Role and Function of the Instructional Materials Center," *Instructional Materials Center*, ed. Neville B. Pearson and Lucius Butler (Minneapolis: Burgess Publishing Company, 1969), p. 341.
5. "Guidelines for Two-Year College Learning Resources Programs," *College and Research Libraries News*, XXX (December, 1972), p. 309. Also found in *Audiovisual Instruction*, XVIII (January, 1973), p. 55.
6. American Library Association and National Education Association, *Standards for School Media Programs* (Chicago: American Library Association and National Education Association, 1969), p. 2.
7. Trevor Duprey, *Modern Libraries for Modern Colleges* (Washington: Communication Service Corporation, 1968), p. 48.
8. James Brown and Kenneth Norberg, *Administering Educational Media* (New York: McGraw-Hill Book Company, 1965), p. 10.
9. Len Singer, "Florida Atlantic University: "Where Tomorrow Begins," *Audiovisual Instruction*, VIII (April, 1963), p. 237.
10. B. Lamar Johnson, "Vitalizing a College Library; A Quarter Century Later," *The Junior College Library*, ed. B. Lamar Johnson, Occasional Report Number 8 (Los Angeles: University of California, 1965), p. 29.
11. T. N. Duprey, Ferment in College Libraries; *The Impact of Information Technology* (Washington: Communication Service Corporation, 1968), p. 59.
12. Fred Harcleroad, "Learning Resources Approach to Library Development," *Library Trends*, XVI (October, 1967), pp. 238-239.

Notes to Chapter III

1. J. W. Getzels and E. G. Guba, "Social Behavior and the Administrative Process," *The School Review*, LXV (Winter, 1957), p. 430.
2. John W. Gardner, *Excellence* (New York: Harper & Row, Publishers, 1961), p. 136.
3. Harold Koontz and Cyril O'Donnell, *Principles of Management* (New York: McGraw-Hill Book Company, Inc., 1964), p. 4.
4. Ibid., pp. 18-19.
5. William B. Castetter, *Administering the School Personnel Program* (New York: The Macmillan Company, 1962), p. 63.

6. Ibid., p. 69.

7. Edward T. Hall, *The Silent Language* (New York: Doubleday and Company, Inc., 1959), p. 52.

8. Lyle, *The Administration of the College Library*, p. 180.

9. Philip Lewis, "The Role of the Educational Communications Specialists," *American School Board Journal*, CXLIII (December, 1961), p. 17.

10. James W. Brown, "AV and Library: Complement or Merge?" *Educational Screen and Audiovisual Guide*, XLVI (January, 1967), p. 23.

11. C. Walter Stone, "The Library Function Redefined," *Library Trends*, XVI (October, 1967), pp. 182-183.

12. Raymond Wyman, "The Instructional Materials Center: Whose Empire?" *Audiovisual Instruction*, XII (February, 1967), p. 116.

13. C. Walter Stone, "AV Task Force Survey Report," *American Libraries*, I (January, 1970), p. 43.

14. Raymond Wyman, "An Interdisciplinary Approach to Planning a Program of Professional Preparation for Media Specialists," *Audiovisual Instruction*, XII (February, 1967), p. 113.

15. Norman E. Tanis, "Education for Junior College Librarianship," *Junior College Libraries Development, Needs and Perspectives*, ed. Everett Moore (Chicago: American Library Association, 1969), p. 76.

16. Lester E. Asheim, "Education and Manpower for Librarianship," *ALA Bulletin*, XLII (October, 1968), p. 1096.

17. Jim Wallington, Pryor Hale, and Freda Douglas, "Toward Solving the Media Manpower Puzzle," *Audiovisual Instruction*, XIV (January, 1969), p. 36.

18. Sherwin G. Swartout, "Professional or Paraprofessional?" *Audiovisual Instruction*, XII (February, 1967), p. 131.

19. James W. Brown, "The New Joint Standards: Implications for Manpower," *Audiovisual Instruction*, XIV (January, 1969), p. 33.

20. Asheim, "Education and Manpower for Librarianship," p. 1104.

21. Ibid., p. 1099.

22. Fritz Veit, "Training the Junior College Librarian," *Journal of Education for Librarianship*, IX (Fall, 1968), p. 113.

23. Joseph Wheeler and Herbert Goldhor, *Practical Administration of Public Libraries* (New York: Harper & Row, 1962), p. 72.

24. Elizabeth Martin and others, "Junior College Library Personnel Needs, Reports of a Survey, 1966-67" (unpublished Junior College Libraries Section, Association of College and Research Libraries, 1967), n.p.

25. Louis Shores, "The Junior College Impact in Academic Librarianship," *College and Research Libraries*, XXX (May, 1969), p. 219.

26. Fritz Veit, "Job Descriptions for Library Technical Assistants" (Chicago: Council on Library Technology, 1970), p. 25. (Mimeographed.)

27. Bill F. Grady, "The Preparation and Certification of Educational Media Personnel," *Audiovisual Instruction*, XIV (January, 1969), p. 29.

28. Joseph W. Gilkey, "The Media Numbers Game," *Audiovisual Instruction*, XIV (September, 1969), p. 50.

29. Dale Hamreus, "Media Guidelines," *Audiovisual Instruction*, XV (May, 1970), p. 32.

30. Carlton Erickson, "The Making of New School Media Specialists—From the Audio-visual Point of View," *Audiovisual Instruction,* XIV (January, 1969), pp. 17-19.
31. William H. King, "The Emerging Role of the Instructional Materials Specialist," *Audiovisual Instruction,* XIV (September, 1969), p. 27.
32. Vernon Bronson, "Professional Training of Personnel for Educational Television," *Audiovisual Instruction,* XIV (January, 1969), p. 40.
33. Richard S. Meyers, "Money and Morale," *Audiovisual Instruction,* XV (May, 1970), p. 73.
34. Elwood Miller, "Proposed: A Media Clerk-Technician," *Audiovisual Instruction,* IX (November, 1964), p. 607.
35. Richard S. Meyers, "Community College Media Technology Program," *Audiovisual Instruction,* XIV (September, 1969), p. 62.
36. Amo DeBernardis, "The New Challenge for Community Colleges," *Educational Screen and Audiovisual Guide,* XLIV (December, 1965), p. 35.

Notes to Chapter IV

1. Guy R. Lyle, *The Administration of the College Library,* p. 320.
2. James W. Brown and Kenneth P. Norberg, *Administering Educational Media* (New York: McGraw-Hill Book Company, 1965), p. 160.
3. Lyle, op.cit., pp. 325-328.
4. Maurice F. Tauber and Irene Roemer Stephens (eds.), *Library Survey* (New York: Columbia University Press, 1967), p. 117.
5. Ibid., p. 98.
6. *Standards and Criteria for the Evaluation and Recognition of Illinois Public Junior Colleges and Other Guidelines, Policies and Procedures Approved by the Illinois Junior College Board* (Springfield: Illinois Junior College Board, 1967), p. 16.
7. "Guidelines for Two-Year College Learning Resources Programs," p. 310.
8. Illinois Library Association, *A Multimedia Survey of the Community College Libraries of the State of Illinois,* pp. 2, 12, 13.
9. Association of College and Research Libraries, *Monograph,* No. 20 (1958), p. 14.
10. Lyle, op. cit., p. 333.
11. Fred J. Heinritz, "Quantitative Management in Libraries," *College and Research Libraries,* XXX (July, 1970), p. 236.
12. Roy Jordan, "Clarifying an AV Budget," *Audiovisual Instruction,* XV (May, 1970), p. 69.

Notes to Chapter V

1. "Guidelines for Two-Year College Learning Resources Programs," p. 313.
2. Guy R. Lyle, *The President, The Professor, and The College Library* (New York: The H. W. Wilson Company, 1963), p. 40.
3. Carlton Erickson, *Fundamentals of Teaching with Audiovisual Technology* (New York: The Macmillan Company, 1965), pp. 98-99.
4. Lyle, *Administration of the College Library,* p. 399.

5. Peggy Sullivan, "Junior College Libraries as Seen in Student Handbooks," *PNLA Quarterly*, XXXIII (Fall, 1969), p. 10.

6. Verner W. Clapp and Robert T. Jordan, "Quantitative Criteria for Adequacy of Academic Library Collections," *College and Research Libraries*, XXVI (September, 1965), p. 373.

7. Lyle, op. cit., p. 238.

8. David O. Lane, "The Selection of Academic Library Materials, A Literature Survey," *College and Research Libraries*, XXVIII (September, 1968), p. 364.

9. Ibid., p. 371.

10. C. James Schmidt, "Administering the Book Budget: A Survey of State Supported Academic Libraries in Texas," *Texas Library Journal*, XLII (Summer, 1966), p. 51.

11. Harvie Branscomb, *Teaching with Books* (Hamden, Connecticut: The Shoe String Press, Inc., 1964), pp. 185-194.

12. Robert Haro, "Book Selection in Academic Libraries," *College and Research Libraries*, XXVIII (March, 1967), p. 104.

13. Alfredo Guadalupe de los Santos, Jr., "Book Selection Factors and the Nature of the Junior College Library" (unpublished dissertation, The University of Texas, 1965).

14. Harry Bach, "Acquisition Policy in the American Academic Library," *College and Research Libraries*, XVIII (November, 1957), p. 447.

15. Bonnie J. Mitchell, John White and Alice B. Griffith, "Junior College Materials," *Choice*, VI (March, 1969), pp. 28-29.

16. Ibid., p. 30.

17. John F. Harvey, "The Role of the Junior College Library," *College and Research Libraries*, XXVII (May, 1966), p. 229.

18. "Guidelines for Two-Year College Learning Resources Programs," p. 313.

19. American Library Association, *Library Bill of Rights*, adopted June 27, 1967.

20. Humphrey A. Olsen, "Building the Book Collection," *Library Trends*, XIV (October, 1965), p. 163.

21. Alice B. Griffith, "Building the Quality Book Collection," *Junior College Journal*, XL (June-July, 1970), p. 18.

22. Ibid.

23. Sullivan, "Junior College Libraries as Seen in Student Handbooks," p. 10.

24. Charles Joseph Bensen, "Study of the Student Use of Periodicals in a Junior College Library" (unpublished Master's thesis, University of Chicago, 1955), p. 67.

25. Horace C. Hartsel and R. A. Margoles, "Guidelines for the Selection of Instructional Materials," *Audiovisual Instruction*, XII (January, 1967), p. 26.

26. Jerrold E. Kemp, *Planning and Producing Audiovisual Materials* (San Francisco: Chandler Publishing Company, 1968), p. 6.

27. Mary Ellen Oliverio, "Selecting Instructional Materials for the Classroom," *Balance Sheet*, XLVII (December, 1965), p. 169.

28. Carlton Erickson, *Fundamentals of Teaching with Audiovisual Technology*, p. 100.

29. Ibid., p. 95.

30. George E. Rollins, "How We Select Materials and Equipment," *Audiovisual Instruction*, XIV (May, 1969), p. 38.

31. Erickson, op. cit., p. 83.

32. Ibid., p. 84.

33. Ibid., pp. 85-86.

Notes to Chapter VI

1. Maurice F. Tauber, *Technical Services in Libraries* (New York: Columbia University Press, 1965), p. 9.
2. E. J. Josey, "Significance of the Findings to Junior College Libraries," *College and Research Libraries,* XXXI (May, 1970), p. 196.
3. Leontine D. Carroll, "Students Don't Need the Library," *Improving College and University Teaching,* XII (Spring, 1964), p. 81.
4. Sister Helen Sheehan, "Students and the Library," *Drexel Library Quarterly,* IV (January, 1968), p. 45.
5. Ibid., pp. 47-49.
6. William H. Carlson, "Measures of Library Excellence," *Improving College and University Teaching,* XII (Spring, 1964), p. 69.
7. Richard W. Hostrop, *Teaching and the Community College Library* (Hamden, Conn.: The Shoe String Press, 1968), pp. 162-165.
8. Kenneth Allen, *Use of Community College Libraries* (Hamden, Conn.: The Shoe String Press, 1971).
9. Howard Clayton, "An Investigation of Various Social and Economic Factors Influencing Student Use of One College Library" (Unpublished Doctor's dissertation, The University of Oklahoma, 1965), pp. 107-116.
10. Patricia B. Knapp, *College Teaching and the College Library*, American College and Research Libraries Monograph Number 23 (New York: American Library Association, 1959), pp. 29, 92-93.
11. Patricia B. Knapp, "College Teaching and the Library," *Illinois Libraries,* XL (December, 1958), pp. 828-831.
12. Harvie Branscomb, *Teaching with Books: A Study of College Libraries,* p. 39.
13. Virginia Clark, "Student Use of a Junior College Library," *Illinois Libraries,* XL (May, 1960), pp. 316-318.
14. Andrew H. Horn and others, "Report of a Brief Survey of the El Camino Library" (El Camino College, El Camino, California, 1966), pp. 30-77.
15. Gorham Lane, "Assessing the Undergraduates' Use of the University Library," *College and Research Libraries,* XXVII (July, 1966), pp. 277-282.
16. Orlando Behling and Kermit Cudd, "A Library Looks at Itself," *College and Research Libraries,* XXVIII (November, 1967), pp. 416-422.
17. A. K. Jain, "Sampling and Short-Period Usage in the Purdue Library," *College and Research Libraries,* XXVII (May, 1966), pp. 211-218.
18. Charles Alexander, A Conference on the Administration of Library Instructional Services in the Community College, Highlights of a Conference (Detroit: Wayne State University, 1965), p. 26.
19. Arthur Roy Rowland, "Cataloging and Classification in Junior College Libraries," *Library Resources and Technical Services,* VII (Summer, 1963), p. 255.
20. Peggy Sullivan, "Junior College Libraries as Seen in Student Handbooks," p. 9.
21. Richard H. Schimmelpfeng and C. Donald Cook (eds.), *The Use of the Library of Congress Classification* (Chicago: American Library Association, 1968), pp. 209-220.

22. R. E. Holdridge, "Cataloging Non-book Materials," *Audiovisual Instruction,* XII (April, 1967), p. 358.

23. Department of Audiovisual Instruction, *Standards for Cataloging, Coding and Scheduling Educational Media* (Washington: National Education Association, 1968), p. iii.

24. Louis H. Brown, "Retrieving Media Information According to Content on Subject Area," *Audiovisual Instruction,* XIV (February, 1969), pp. 73-74.

25. William J. Quinly, "Computerized Cataloging," *Audiovisual Instruction,* XII (April, 1967), p. 321.

26. Christopher Barnes, "Classification and Cataloging of Spoken Records in Academic Libraries," *College and Research Libraries,* XXVIII (January, 1967), p. 49.

27. Tauber, *Technical Services in Libraries,* p. 118.

28. Robert M. Hayes, Ralph M. Shoffner, and David Weber, "The Economics of Book Catalog Production," *Library Resources and Technical Services,* X (Winter, 1966), pp. 58-59.

29. James W. Pirie, "Junior College Library Processing," *Library Trends,* XIV (October, 1965), p. 166.

30. Jesse H. Shera, *Documentation and the Organization of Knowledge* (London: Crosby Lockwood and Hamden: The Shoe String Press, Inc., 1966), p. 176.

31. Allen B. Veaner, "Major Decision Points in Library Automation," *College and Research Libraries,* XXX (September, 1970), pp. 299-300.

32. Henrietta Avram, "MARC is a Four-Letter-Word—Machine Readable Cataloging," *Library Journal,* XCIII (July, 1968), pp. 2601-2605.

33. Eleanor G. Eyman and others, "Periodicals Automation at Miami-Date Junior College," *Library Resources and Technical Services,* X (Summer, 1966), p. 242.

34. Ralph Parker, "Economic Considerations," *Data Processing in University Libraries,* ed. John Harvey (Washington: Spartan Books, 1966), p. 147.

35. Joseph Beaker, "The Future of Library Automation and Information Networks," *Library Automation: A State of the Art Review,* ed. Stephen R. Salmon (Chicago: American Library Association, 1969), p. 6.

36. Carl Hodge, "EDUCOM," *Audiovisual Instruction,* XII (April, 1967), p. 352.

Notes to Chapter VII

1. Agnes Stein, "What is a Librarian?" *Wilson Library Bulletin,* XLI (April, 1967), p. 781.

2. Neal Harlow, "Newes of the New Founde Worlde," *Library Journal,* XXCVIII (June 1, 1963), p. 2193.

3. Patricia Gebhard, "School for Ninety-Day Wonders," *Library Journal,* XXCVIII (June 1, 1963), p. 2200.

4. Jane W. Daniels, "Aid Through Aides," *Library Journal,* XXCVIII (June 1, 1963), p. 2195.

5. U. S. Department of Labor, *Occupational Outlook Handbook 1972-73 Edition* (Washington, D. C.: U. S. Government Printing Office, 1972), pp. 253-254.

6. The Library Technical Assistant Program, *Guidelines and Course Content for Community College Programs* (Sacramento, California: Office of the Chancellor, California Community Colleges, July, 1970), p. 8.

7. Council on Library Technology, *Newsletter,* Vol. 2, No. 3 (June, 1969), p. 1.

8. Ibid., p. 2.
9. John Martinson, *Vocational Training for Library Technicians: A Survey of Experience to Date* (Washington, D. C.: Communications Service Corporation, 1965), p. 1.
10. Ibid., p. 2.
11. Council on Library Technology, *Newsletter,* Vol. 2, No. 1 (January, 1969), pp. 1-3.
12. California Community Colleges Chancellor's Office, *Survey of Library Technical Assistant Program,* March, 1969, p. 3.
13. American Library Association, Education Division, *Newsletter,* No. 53 (March, 1965), p. 35.
14. D. F. Deiniger, *Report of Joint Ad Hoc Committee of Library Administration Division & Library Education Division on Subprofessional or Technician Class of Library Employees,* American Library Association, 1967.
15. Council on Library Technology, *Newsletter,* Vol. 1, No. 2 (May, 1968), p. 2.
16. California State Department of Education, *Multi-Media and the Changing School Library* (Sacramento: California State Department of Education, 1959), pp. 59-60.
17. Samuel Sass, "Library Technicians—Instant Librarians?" *Library Journal,* XCII (June 1, 1967), p. 2122.
18. *Staff Analysis and Recommendations* for the Coordinating Council for Higher Education Meeting of July 15, 1969, San Francisco, California.
19. Council on Library Technology, *Newsletter,* Vol. 1, No. 3 (July, 1968), p. 3.
20. American Library Association, "Criteria for Programs to Prepare Library Technical Assistant" *(*Chicago: American Library Association, January, 1969). (Mimeographed.)
21. "A Viable Curriculum for Library Technology," *California School Libraries* (Sacramento, California, 1969), p. 21.
22. Council on Library Technology, *Newsletter,* Vol. 1, No. 2 (May, 1968), p. 3.
23. Office of the Chancellor, The California Community Colleges, *The Library Technical Assistant Program, Guidelines and Course Content for Community College Programs* (Sacramento, California), p. 1.
24. Ibid., p. 3.
25. American Library Association, *The Subprofessional or Technical Assistant; A Statement of Definition* (Chicago, Illinois: April, 1968), p. 395.
26. American Library Association, Library Education Division, "Criteria for Programs to Prepare Library Technical Assistants," *ALA Bulletin,* LXIII (June, 1969), pp. 787-794.
27. U. S. Civil Service Commission, "Position Classification Standards for GS-1411, Library Technician Series" (released under Transmittal 62, June, 1966), p. 2.

Notes to Chapter VIII

1. Martin Van Buren, "Layout Plans and Library Interiors," *Guidelines for Library Planners* (Chicago: American Library Association, 1960), p. 16.
2. U. S. Department of Health, Education, and Welfare, *A Guide for Planning Community Junior College Facilities* (Washington, D. C.: U. S. Printing Office, 1969), p. 14.

3. Keyes D. Metcalf, "The Use of Hindsight in Planning Library Buildings," *Library Buildings for the Future* (Chicago: American Library Association, 1967), p. 8.

4. Keyes D. Metcalf, *Planning Academic and Research Library Buildings* (New York: McGraw-Hill Book Company, 1965), p. 10.

5. Educational Facilities Laboratories, Inc., *Bricks and Mortarboards* (New York: Educational Facilities Laboratories, Inc., 1966), p. 71.

6. Ibid., p. 98.

7. Richard A. Jones, "Building Planning: Design for Unique and Innovative Centers," Selected Papers from Northern Illinois University Community College Conferences, 1967-1968, p. 81.

8. Alan C. Green and others, *Educational Facilities With New Media* (Washington, D. C.: National Education Association, 1966), p. A-10.

9. Ralph E. Ellsworth and Hobart D. Wagener, *The School Library* (New York: Educational Facilities Laboratories, 1963), p. 20.

10. Elizabeth Martin, *Planning Library Facilities* (Los Altos, California: Foothill College District, January, 1967). (Mimeographed.)

11. Metcalf, *Planning Academic and Research Library Buildings*, p. 87.

12. Ralph E. Ellsworth, *Planning College and University Library Buildings* (Boulder, Colorado: Pruett Press, Inc., 1968), pp. 41-49.

13. Metcalf, *Planning Academic and Research Library Buildings*, pp. 92-94.

14. Green and others, *Educational Facilities With New Media*, p. B-18.

15. Ibid., pp. B-75-76.

16. Educational Facilities Laboratories, *Bricks and Mortarboards*, p. 98.

17. Higher Education Facilities Planning and Management Manuals, *Manual Four, Academic Support Facilities* (Boulder, Colorado: Western Interstate Commission for Higher Education, 1971).

18. Franklin G. Matsler, *Space and Utilization Standards, California Public Higher Education, A Report to the Coordinating Council for Higher Education* (Sacramento, California: Ed 013 079, September, 1966), p. 38.

19. Educational Facilities Laboratories, op. cit., p. 8.

20. Matsler, p. 38.

21. Metcalf, *Planning for Academic and Research Libraries*, pp. 393-395.

22. Matsler, p. 27.

23. Ibid.

24. Ibid., p. 38.

25. Metcalf, *Planning Academic and Research Library Buildings*, p. 132.

26. Higher Education Facilities Planning and Management Manuals, *Academic Support Facilities*, p. 67.

27. American Library Association, "The Use of Carpeting in Libraries," *Library Technology Project* (Chicago: American Library Association, 1962), pp. 1-2.

28. Educational Facilities Laboratories, Inc., *The School Library*, p. 95.

29. American Carpet Institute, *Excellence and Economy* (New York: American Carpet Institute, 1965), p. 35.

30. H. Richard Blackwell, "Lighting the Library—Standards for Illumination," *The Library Environment/Aspects of Interior Planning* (Chicago: American Library Association, 1965), pp. 23-24.

31. Brock Arms, "Principles of Illumination for Libraries," *The Library Environment/*

Aspects of Interior Planning (Chicago: American Library Association, 1965), p. 133.

32. Metcalf, *Planning Academic and Research Library Buildings,* pp. 184-185.
33. Educational Facilities Laboratory, *Bricks and Mortarboards,* pp. 78-80.
34. Robert Sommer, "The Ecology of Privacy," *Library Quarterly,* XXXVI (July, 1966), p. 247.
35. Ellsworth, *Planning the College and University Library Building,* p. 95.
36. J. C. R. Licklider, *Libraries of the Future* (Cambridge, Massachusetts: The M.I.T. Press, 1965), p. 38.
37. Robert H. Blackburn, "Automation and Building Plans," *Library Trends,* XVIII (October, 1969), p. 267.
38. Matsler, p. 39.
39. Green and others, *Educational Facilities With New Media,* p. A-42.
40. Lloyd R. DeGarmo, "Building and Equipment Trends, II," *Library Trends,* XIV (October, 1965), p. 213.

Notes to Chapter IX

1. S. N. Postlethwait, J. Novak, and H. T. Murray, Jr., *The Audio-Tutorial Approach to Learning* (Minneapolis, Minnesota: Burgess Publishing Co. 1969), p. 10.
2. Lee Lebbin, "Library-College to the Point" *The Library-College Omnibus, Vol. 5,* (June, 1972), p. 6.
3. For additional information on this topic, the periodical *Learning Today* and Louis Shores' *Library-College U.S.A.* should be consulted.
4. National Education Association, *Schools for the Sixties* (New York: McGraw-Hill Book Company, 1963), p. 50.
5. Educational Facilities Laboratories, *Bricks and Mortarboards,* p. 72.
6. Edmund M. Midura, "Why Aren't We Getting Through?" *The Urban Communications Crisis* (Acropolis Books, 1971).
7. Daniel Melcher, "Cataloging, Processing, and Automation," *American Libraries* II, No. 7, July, August 1971, p. 701-713.

Bibliography

Alexander, Charles. A Conference on the Administration of Library Instructional Services in the Community College, Highlights of a Conference. Detroit: Wayne State University, 1965.

Allen, Kenneth. *Use of Community College Libraries*. Hamden, Conn.: The Shoe String Press, 1971.

American Association of Junior Colleges. *An Introduction to American Junior Colleges*. Washington, D. C.: American Council on Education, 1967.

American Association of Junior Colleges. *Junior Colleges in 50 States/50 Years*. Washington, D. C.: American Association of Junior Colleges, 1969.

American Association of Junior Colleges. *1972 Junior College Directory*. Washington, D. C.: American Association of Junior Colleges, 1972.

American Association of Junior Colleges and the Association of College and Research Libraries. *Guidelines for Two-Year College Library Learning Resource Centers*. 1972. Mimeographed.

American Carpet Institute. *Excellence and Economy*. New York: American Carpet Institute, 1965.

American College Testing Program, Inc. *The Two-Year College and Its Students: An Empirical Report*. Iowa City, Iowa: The Corporation, 1969.

American Library Association. "Criteria for Programs to Prepare Library Technical Assistants." Chicago: American Library Association, January, 1969. Mimeographed.

American Library Association. *Guidelines for Library Planners*. Chicago: American Library Association, 1960.

American Library Association, American Association of Community and Junior Colleges, Association for Educational Communications and Technology. "Guidelines for Two-year College Learning Resources Programs," *College and Research Libraries News*, XXXIII (Dec. 1972), p. 305-315. Also found in *Audiovisual Instruction* XVIII (January, 1973), p. 50-61.

American Library Association, *Library Bill of Rights*. Adopted June 27, 1967.

American Library Association. *Library Buildings for the Future*. Chicago: American Library Association, 1967.

American Library Association, Education Division. *Newsletter*, No. 53 (March, 1965).

American Library Association, Library Education Division. "Criteria for Programs to Prepare Library Technical Assistants," *ALA Bulletin*, LXIII (June, 1969), 787-794.

American Library Association. *The Library Environment/Aspects of Interior Planning*. Chicago: American Library Association, 1965.

American Library Association and National Education Association. *Standards for School Media Programs*. Chicago: American Library Association and National Education Association, 1969.

American Library Association. "Standards for Junior College Libraries," *College and*

Research Libraries, XXI (May, 1960), 200-206.

American Library Association. *The Subprofessional or Technical Assistant; A Statement of Definition.* Chicago, Illinois. April, 1968.

American Library Association. "The Use of Carpeting in Libraries," *Library Technology Project.* Chicago: American Library Association, 1962.

Asheim, Lester E. "Education and Manpower for Librarianship," *ALA Bulletin,* XLII (October, 1968), 1096-1105.

Association of College and Research Libraries. *Monograph,* No. 20 (1958).

Association for Supervision and Curriculum Development. *Perceiving, Behaving, Becoming: A New Focus.* Washington, D. C.: National Education Association, 1962.

Avram, Henrietta. "MARC is a Four-Letter-Word—Machine Readable Cataloging," *Library Journal,* XCIII (July, 1968), 2601-2605.

Bach, Harry. "Acquisition Policy in the American Academic Library," *College and Research Libraries,* XVIII (November, 1957), 441-452.

Barnes, Christopher. "Classification and Cataloging of Spoken Records in Academic Libraries," *College and Research Libraries,* XXVIII (January, 1967), 49-52.

Behling, Orlando, and Kermit Cudd. "A Library Looks at Itself," *College and Research Libraries,* XXVIII (November, 1967), 416-422.

Bensen, Charles Joseph. "Study of the Student Use of Periodicals in a Junior College Library." Unpublished Master's thesis, University of Chicago, 1955.

Blackburn, Robert H. "Automation and Building Plans," *Library Trends,* XVIII (October, 1969), 262-267.

Blocker, Clyde E., Robert H. Plummer, and Richard C. Richardson, Jr. *The Two-year College: A Social Synthesis.* Englewood Cliffs, New Jersey: Prentice-Hall, Inc., 1965.

Branscomb, Harvie. *Teaching with Books.* Hamden, Connecticut: The Shoe String Press, Inc., 1964.

Bronson, Vernon. "Professional Training of Personnel for Educational Television," *Audiovisual Instruction,* XIV (January, 1969), 38-40.

Brown, James W. "AV and Library: Complement or Merge?" *Educational Screen and Audiovisual Guide,* XLVI (January, 1967), 22-23.

Brown, James W. "The New Joint Standards: Implications for Manpower," *Audiovisual Instruction,* XIV (January, 1969), 31-33.

Brown, James, and Kenneth Norberg. *Administering Educational Media.* New York: McGraw-Hill Book Company, 1965.

Brown, Louis H. "Retrieving Media Information According to Content on Subject Area," *Audiovisual Instruction,* XIV (February, 1969), 71-74.

California State Department of Education. *Multi-Media and the Changing School Library.* Sacramento: California State Department of Education, 1959.

Carlson, William H. "Measures of Library Excellence," *Improving College and University Teaching,* XII (Spring, 1964), 68-69.

The Carnegie Commission on Higher Education. *The Open-Door Colleges.* New York: McGraw-Hill Book Company, 1970.

Carroll, Leontine D. "Students Don't Need the Library," *Improving College and University Teaching,* XII (Spring, 1964), 81-82.

Castetter, William B. *Administering the School Personnel Program.* New York: The Macmillan Company, 1962.

Clapp, Verner W., and Robert T. Jordan. "Quantitative Criteria for Adequacy of Academic Library Collections," *College and Research Libraries,* XXVI (September, 1965), 371-380.

Clark, Virginia. "Student Use of a Junior College Library," *Illinois Libraries,* XL (May, 1960), 316-318.

Clayton, Howard. "An Investigation of Various Social and Economic Factors Influencing Student Use of One College Library." Unpublished Doctor's dissertation, The University of Oklahoma, 1965.

Cohen, Arthur M. and Florence B. Brower. *Confronting Identity: The Community College Instructor.* Englewood Cliffs, New Jersey: Prentice-Hall, Inc., 1972.

Council on Library Technology. *Newsletter,* Vol. 1, No. 2 (May, 1968).

Council on Library Technology. *Newsletter,* Vol. 1, No. 3 (July, 1968).

Council on Library Technology. *Newsletter,* Vol. 2, No. 1 (January, 1969).

Council on Library Technology. *Newsletter,* Vol. 2, No. 3 (June, 1969).

Cross, Patricia. *The Junior College Student: A Research Description.* Princeton, New Jersey: Educational Testing Service, 1968.

Daniels, Jane W. "Aid Through Aides," *Library Journal,* LXXXVIII (June 1, 1963), 2194-2197.

DeBernardis, Amo. "The New Challenge for Community Colleges," *Educational Screen and Audiovisual Guide,* XLIV (December, 1965), 34-35.

DeGarmo, Lloyd R. "Building and Equipment Trends," *Library Trends,* XIV (October, 1965), 209-215.

Deiniger, D. F. *Report of Joint Ad Hoc Committee of Library Administration Division & Library Education Division of Subprofessional or Technician Class of Library Employees.* Chicago: American Library Association, 1967.

DeNure, Mary E. "A Viable Curriculum for Library Technician Programs," *California School Libraries,* XXXIX (November, 1967), 18-25.

Department of Audiovisual Instruction. *Standards for Cataloging, Coding and Scheduling Educational Media.* Washington, D. C.: National Education Association, 1968.

Duprey, T. N. *Ferment in College Libraries; The Impact of Information Technology.* Washington, D. C.: Communication Service Corporation, 1968.

Duprey, Trevor. *Modern Libraries for Modern Colleges.* Washington, D. C.: Communication Service Corporation, 1968.

Educational Facilities Laboratories. *Bricks and Mortarboards.* New York: Educational Facilities Laboratories, 1966.

Ellsworth, Ralph E. *Planning College and University Library Buildings.* Boulder, Colorado: Pruett Press, Inc., 1968.

Ellsworth, Ralph E., and Hobart D. Wagener. *The School Library.* New York: Educational Facilities Laboratories, 1963.

Erickson, Carlton. *Fundamentals of Teaching with Audiovisual Technology.* New York: The Macmillan Company, 1965.

Erickson, Carlton. "The Making of New School Media Specialists—From the Audiovisual Point of View," *Audiovisual Instruction,* XIV (January, 1969), 15-19.

Eyman, Eleanor G., and others. "Periodicals Automation at Miami-Dade Junior College," *Library Resources and Technical Services,* X (Summer, 1966), 341-362.

Gardner, John W. *Excellence*. New York: Harper & Row, Publishers, 1961.

Gebhard, Patricia. "School for Ninety-Day Wonders," *Library Journal*, LXXXVIII (June 1, 1963), 2198-2200.

Getzels, J. W., and E. G. Guba. "Social Behavior and the Administrative Process," *The School Review*, LXV (Winter, 1957), 423-441.

Gilkey, Joseph W. "The Media Numbers Game," *Audiovisual Instruction*, XIV (September, 1969), 49-50.

Gleazer, Edmund. *This is the Community College*. Boston: Houghton Mifflin, 1968.

Grady, Bill F. "The Preparation and Certification of Educational Media Personnel," *Audiovisual Instruction*, XIV (January, 1969), 29-30.

Green, Alan C., and others. *Educational Facilities with New Media*. Washington, D.C.: National Education Association, 1966.

Griffith, Alice B. "Building the Quality Book Collection," *Junior College Journal*, XL (June-July, 1970), 16-20.

Hall, Edward T. *The Silent Language*. New York: Doubleday and Company, Inc., 1959.

Hamreus, Dale. "Media Guidelines," *Audiovisual Instruction*, XV (May, 1970), 31-34.

Harcleroad, Fred. "Learning Resources Approach to Library Development," *Library Trends*, XVI (October, 1967), 228-240.

Harlow, Neal. "Newes of the New Founde Worlde," *Library Journal*, XXCVIII (June 1, 1963), 2189-2193.

Haro, Robert. "Book Selection in Academic Libraries," *College and Research Libraries*, XXVIII (March, 1967), 104-106.

Hartsell, Horace C., and R. A. Margoles. "Guidelines for the Selection of Instructional Materials," *Audiovisual Instruction*, XII (January, 1967), 26.

Harvey, John (ed.). *Data Processing in University Libraries*. Washington, D. C.: Spartan Books, 1966.

Harvey, John F. "The Role of the Junior College Library," *College and Research Libraries*, XXVII (May, 1966), 229-230.

Hayes, Robert M., Ralph M. Shoffner, and David Weber. "The Economics of Book Catalog Production," *Library Resources and Technical Services*, X (Winter, 1966), 58-67.

Heinritz, Fred J. "Quantitative Management in Libraries," *College and Research Libraries*, XXX (July, 1970), 232-237.

Hodge, Carl. "EDUCOM," *Audiovisual Instruction*, XII (April, 1967), 352-356.

Holdridge, R. E. "Cataloging Non-book Materials," *Audiovisual Instruction*, XII (April, 1967), 358-360.

Horn, Andrew H., and others. "Report of a Brief Survey of the El Camino College Library." El Camino, California: El Camino College, 1966.

Hostrop, Richard W. *Teaching and the Community College Library*. Hamden, Connecticut: The Shoe String Press, 1968.

Illinois Junior College Board. *Report of Selected Data and Characteristics: Illinois Public Colleges, 1970-71*. Springfield: Illinois Junior College Board, 1971.

Illinois Library Association. *A Multimedia Survey of the Community College Libraries of the State of Illinois*. Springfield: Illinois Library Association, 1969.

Illinois Revised Statutes. *Illinois Public Junior College Act*. Chapter 122: Sections 101-1 to 108-2, 1969.

Jain, A. K. "Sampling and Short-Period Usage in the Purdue Library," *College and Research Libraries,* XXVII (May, 1966), 211-218.

Johnson, B. Lamar (ed.). *The Junior College Library,* Occasional Report Number 8. Los Angeles: University of California, 1965.

Johnson, B. Lamar. "Needed: Experimental Junior Colleges," *Junior College Journal,* XXXVI (October, 1965), 17-20.

Jones, Richard A. "Building Planning: Design for Unique and Innovative Centers." Selected Papers from Northern Illinois University Community College Conferences, 1967-1968. (Mimeographed.)

Jordan, Roy. "Clarifying an AV Budget," *Audiovisual Instruction,* XV (May, 1970), 69-71.

Josey, E. J. "Significance of the Findings to Junior College Libraries," *College and Research Libraries,* XXXI (May, 1970), 196.

Kelly, Win, and Leslie Wilbur. *Teaching in the Community Junior College.* New York: Appleton-Century-Crofts, 1970.

Kemp, Jerrold E. *Planning and Producing Audiovisual Materials.* San Francisco: Chandler Publishing Company, 1968.

King, William H. "The Emerging Role of the Instructional Materials Specialist," *Audiovisual Instruction,* XIV (September, 1969), 27-28.

Knapp, Patricia B. *College Teaching and the College Library,* American College and Research Libraries Monograph Number 23. New York: American Library Association, 1959.

Knapp, Patricia B. "College Teaching and the Library," *Illinois Libraries,* XL (December, 1958), 828-831.

Koontz, Harold and Cyril O'Donnell. *Principles of Management.* New York: McGraw-Hill Book Company, Inc., 1964.

Lane, David O. "The Selection of Academic Library Materials, A Literature Survey," *College and Research Libraries,* XXVIII (September, 1968), 364-372.

Lane, Gorham. "Assessing the Undergraduates" Use of the University Library," *College and Research Libraries,* XXVII (July, 1966), 277-282.

Lebbin, Lee. "Library-College to the Point," *The Library-College Omnibus,* Vol. 5 (June, 1972), p. 6.

Lewis, Philip. "The Role of the Educational Communications Specialists," *School Board Journal,* CXLIII (December, 1961), 16-17.

Licklider, J. C. R. *Libraries of the Future.* Cambridge, Massachusetts: The M.I.T. Press, 1965.

Lyle, Guy R. *The Administration of the College Library.* New York: H. W. Wilson, 1961.

Lyle, Guy R. *The President, The Professor, and The College Library.* New York: The H. W. Wilson Company, 1963.

Martinson, John. *Vocational Training for Library Technicians: A Survey of Experience to Date.* Washington, D. C.: Communications Service Corporation, 1965.

Matsler, Franklin G. *Space and Utilization Standards, California Public Higher Education, A Report to the Coordinating Council for Higher Education.* Sacramento, California: September, 1966.

McInnis, Noel F. "Students Are a Lot Like People," *Junior College Journal,* XXIX (March, 1968), 40-44.

Medsker, Leland L. *The Junior College: Progress and Prospect.* New York: McGraw-Hill Book Company, 1960.

Melcher, David. "Cataloging, Processing, and Automation," *American Libraries* (July, August, 1971), 701-713.

Metcalf, Keyes D. *Planning Academic and Research Library Buildings.* New York: McGraw-Hill Book Company, 1965.

Meyers, Richard S. "Community College Media Technology Program," *Audiovisual Instruction,* XIV (September, 1969), 62-64.

Meyers, Richard S. "Money and Morale," *Audiovisual Instruction,* XV (May, 1970), 72-73.

Miller, Elwood. "Proposed: A Media Clerk-Technician," *Audiovisual Instruction,* IX (November, 1964), 606-607.

Mitchell, Bonnie J., John White, and Alice B. Griffith. "Junior College Materials," *Choice,* VI (March, 1969), 28-33.

Moore, Everett (ed.). *Junior College Libraries Development, Needs and Perspectives.* Chicago: American Library Association, 1969.

National Education Association. *Schools for the Sixties.* New York: McGraw-Hill Book Company, 1963.

National Education Association, Research Division. *Teacher Supply and Demand in Universities, Colleges, and Junior Colleges, 1963-64 and 1964-65.* Washington, D. C.: National Education Association, 1965.

Office of the Chancellor, California Community Colleges. *The Library Technical Assistant Program, Guidelines and Course Content for Community College Programs.* Sacramento, California: Office of the Chancellor, California Community Colleges, July, 1970.

Office of the Chancellor, California Community Colleges. The *Library Technical Assistant Program, Guidelines and Course Content for Community College Programs.* Sacramento, California: Office of the Chancellor, California Community Colleges, March, 1969.

Oliverio, Mary Ellen. "Selecting Instructional Materials for the Classroom," *Balance Sheet,* XLVII (December, 1965), 169.

Olsen, Humphrey A. "Building the Book Collection," *Library Trends,* XIV (October, 1965), 156-165.

Pearson, Neville B., and Lucius Butler (eds.). *Instructional Materials Center.* Minneapolis: Burgess Publishing Company, 1969.

Pirie, James W. "Junior College Library Processing," *Library Trends,* XIV (October, 1965), 166-173.

Postlethwait, S. N., J. Novak, and H. T. Murray, Jr. *The Audio-Tutorial Approach to Learning.* Minneapolis, Minnesota: Burgess Publishing Company, 1969.

Quinly, William J. "Computerized Cataloging," *Audiovisual Instruction,* XII (April, 1967), 321.

Rollins, George E. "How We Select Materials and Equipment," *Audiovisual Instruction,* XIV (May, 1969), 36-38.

Rowland, Arthur Roy. "Cataloging and Classification in Junior College Libraries," *Library Resources and Technical Services,* VII (Summer, 1963), 254-258.

Salmon, Stephen R. (ed.). *Library Automation: A State of the Art Review.* Chicago: American Library Association, 1969.

Sass, Samuel. "Library Technicians—Instant Librarians?" *Library Journal,* XCII (June 1, 1967), 2122-2126.

de los Santos, Alfredo, Jr. "Book Selection Factors and the Nature of the Junior College Library." Unpublished dissertation, The University of Texas, 1965.

Schimmelpfeng, Richard H., and C. Donald Cook (eds.). *The Use of the Library of Congress Classification.* Chicago: American Library Association, 1968.

Schmidt, C. James. "Administering the Book Budget: A Survey of State Supported Academic Libraries in Texas," *Texas Library Journal,* XLII (Summer, 1966), 51-54.

Schultheiss, Louis A., Don S. Culbertson, and Edward M. Heiliger. *Advanced Data Processing in the University Library.* New York: Scarecrow Press, 1962.

Sheehan, Sister Helen. "Students and the Library," *Drexel Library Quarterly,* IV (January, 1968), 45-49.

Shera, Jesse H. *Documentation and the Organization of Knowledge.* London: Crosby Lockwood, and Hamden, Conn.: Archon Books, 1966.

Shores, Louis. "The Junior College Impact on Academic Librarianship," *College and Research Libraries,* XXX (May, 1969), 214-221.

Shores, Louis. "The Library Junior College," *Junior College Journal,* XXXVI (March, 1966), 6-9.

Singer, Len. "Florida Atlantic University: Where Tomorrow Begins," *Audiovisual Instruction,* VIII (April, 1963), 236-242.

Sommer, Robert. "The Ecology of Privacy," *Library Quarterly,* XXXVI (July, 1966), 234-248.

Staff Analysis and Recommendations for the Coordinating Council for Higher Education Meeting of July 15, 1969, San Francisco, California.

Standards and Criteria for the Evaluation and Recognition of Illinois Public Junior Colleges and Other Guidelines, Policies and Procedures Approved by the Illinois Junior College Board. Springfield: Illinois Junior College Board, 1967.

Stein, Agnes. "What is a Librarian?" *Wilson Library Bulletin,* XLI (April, 1967), 781.

Stone, C. Walter. "AV Task Force Survey Report," *American Libraries,* I (January, 1970), 40-45.

Stone, C. Walter. "The Library Function Redefined," *Library Trends,* XVI (October, 1967), 181-197.

Sullivan, Peggy. "Junior College Libraries as Seen in Student Handbooks," *PNLA Quarterly,* XXXIII (Fall, 1969), 9-13.

Swartout, Sherwin G. "Professional or Paraprofessional?" *Audiovisual Instruction,* XII (February, 1967), 126-131.

Tauber, Maurice F. *Technical Services in Libraries.* New York: Columbia University Press, 1965.

Tauber, Maurice F., and Irene Roemer Stephens (eds.). *Library Survey.* New York: Columbia University Press, 1967.

Thornton, James W. *The Community Junior College.* New York: John Wiley, 1966.

U. S. Civil Service Commission. "Position Classification Standards for GS-1411, Library Technician Series." Released under Transmittal 62, June, 1966.

U. S. Department of Health, Education, and Welfare. *A Guide for Planning Community Junior College Facilities.* Washington, D. C.: U. S. Printing Office, 1969.

U. S. Department of Labor. *Occupational Outlook Handbook 1972-73 Edition.* Washington, D. C.: U. S. Government Printing Office, 1972.

Veaner, Allen B. "Major Decision Points in Library Automation," *College and Research Libraries,* XXX (September, 1970), 299-312.

Veit, Fritz. "Job Descriptions for Library Technical Assistants." Chicago: Council on Library Technology, 1970. (Mimeographed.)

Veit, Fritz. "Training the Junior College Librarian," *Journal of Education for Librarianship,* IX (Fall, 1968), 108-116.

Wallington, Jim, Pryor Hale, and Freda Douglas. "Toward Solving the Media Manpower Puzzle," *Audiovisual Instruction,* XIV (January, 1969), 36-37.

Western Interstate Commission for Higher Education. *Academic Support Facilities, Manual Four.* Boulder, Colorado: 1971.

Wheeler, Joseph, and Herbert Goldhor. *Practical Administration of Public Libraries.* New York: Harper and Row, 1962.

Wyman, Raymond. "An Interdisciplinary Approach to Planning a Program of Professional Preparation for Media Specialists," *Audiovisual Instruction,* XII (February, 1967), 110-113.

Wyman, Raymond. "The Instructional Materials Center: Whose Empire?" *Audiovisual Instruction,* XII (February, 1967), 114-116.

Index